WINNER'S GUIDE TO
OMAHA POKER

D1014292

This book is dedicated with all my brotherly love, understanding, and sympathy to Dan Warren, who plays Omaha in the Olympia, Washington area. Dan, I've looked into it, and in answer to your question, I've determined that yes, they do play Omaha in Omaha.

Special thanks to poker and Omaha newcomer Robert Blaze Barrett of Olathe, Kansas for your incredibly insightful questions and comments. Are you really, really sure you've never player poker before?

Thanks to John "Felonious Maximus" Mioton of Biloxi, Mississippi for your suggestions regarding the chapter on Omaha odds.

And, as always, thank you and all my love to my Olgita, for your proofreading and for letting me be me.

Thanks to comedian and movie star Steve Martin, who fulfilled his purpose in life by influencing my life. Steve, I've never forgotten that in 1977 you said, "I'm looking for one million people to send me one dollar."

The ultimate and final thanks has to be to you, the reader. If you're new to Omaha, never fear. This book will suit you perfectly. If you were to take notes while playing Omaha for the next ten years and then try to arrange those notes into book form, I think this would be your book. If you could go ten years into the future and then come back and tell yourself everything you had learned about Omaha, all you'd have to do is hand yourself this book. It says it all. And for that, you've sent me one dollar, but I've saved you ten years.

Ken Warren, Shawnee, Kansas, March 2003

WINNER'S GUIDE TO
OMAHA POKER

KEN WARREN

CARDOZA PUBLISHING

Cardoza Publishing is the foremost gaming publisher in the world, with a library of over 100 up-to-date and easy-to-read books and strategies. These authoritative works are written by the top experts in their fields and, with more than 6,500,000 books in print, represent the best-selling and most popular gaming books anywhere.

FIRST EDITION

Library of Congress Catalog Card No: 2003100594
ISBN:1-58042-102-4

Visit our new web site (www.cardozapub.com) or write us for a full list of Cardoza books, advanced and computer strategies.

CARDOZA PUBLISHING
P.O. Box 1500, Cooper Station, New York, NY 10276
Phone (800)577-WINS
email: cardozapub@aol.com
www.cardozapub.com

ABOUT THE AUTHOR

After he left the Air Force in 1987, Ken Warren supported himself playing professional Texas hold 'em poker. An excellent tournament player, Warren was asked by several Las Vegas poker rooms to skip their tournaments in order to give other players a chance to win as well. He branched out to Omaha poker, and he's now a consistent winner at both games.

Warren is the best of the new breed of riverboat poker players, and, in fact, has the unique distinction of having played in (and won) the very first legal poker hand dealt in Mississippi in the twentieth century. That landmark hand was kings full of 7s in the big blind position.

Warren is the author of three other books, including the best-selling *Winner's Guide to Texas Hold 'Em Poker*. He makes his home in Shawnee, Kansas.

TABLE OF CONTENTS

1

WELCOME TO OMAHA

The purpose of this book is to teach you how to play Omaha poker in a way that will allow you to be a winner in the long run. I am going to teach you how to play Omaha for high, for low, and then for hi-low split. This book is intended for all levels, so you'll learn to play low limit Omaha. We will not get into pot limit or no limit poker.

The Basic Assumption

Omaha is a great game. You get to hold four cards in your hand. This in turn gives you six separate two-card groupings with which to play your Omaha hand. It might seem that you will always have a hand or a hand to draw to. Folding at any stage of the game will almost always appear to be out of the question. Omaha is, at first, tricky, confusing, and complicated, because of the "two card only" rule. Omaha is to poker what algebra is to simple arithmetic.

I have years of experience teaching people how to play poker, particularly Texas hold 'em. It is unheard of for a player to learn Omaha as his first poker game. Every Omaha player first learns and knows how to play Texas hold 'em before he moves on to Omaha. That's a good thing. Learning to play Texas hold 'em before learning Omaha is like learning to crawl before you learn to walk.

The basic assumption that I'm going to make at the beginning of this book is that you already know how to play Texas hold 'em. Yes, I know what they say about the word assume; however, I'm confident that we're on firm ground here. After I teach you how to deal the game and read the board, we will use Texas hold 'em as our common frame of reference to make the transition to Omaha. I will devote an entire chapter to explaining how Omaha is different from hold 'em.

If you don't know how to play Texas hold 'em, or if you would like to brush up on the game, I recommend either or both of my books on the subject, *Winner's Guide to Texas Hold 'Em* and *Ken Warren Teaches Texas Hold 'Em*, both published by Cardoza Publishing. You can order these books by calling 1-800-577-WINS.

Why Play Omaha?

Because it's exciting, that's why! Each Omaha hand contains six separate hands, and you can play for both high and low hand. It's almost always correct to call more often than in hold 'em, and the pots are always bigger. Plus, the jackpots are easier to hit in Omaha than they are in hold 'em.

There's one reason why you should play Omaha that is more compelling than any of the others: the typical player whose skill might be only mediocre-to-average at hold 'em can be a great player at Omaha. And with less effort! The skills you don't have that are keeping you from being a great hold 'em player aren't all that necessary at Omaha. More about that later.

If you like to play a lot of hands, if you like to be constantly in action, if you like to call more than you like to fold, or if you like to build and win big pots, then Omaha is your game. If you play because you like to earn money at poker, you should know that, given the same stakes and the same level of skill, the Omaha player will make much more money per year than the hold 'em player.

Welcome to Omaha!

2

HOW TO PLAY OMAHA

Betting Limits

Omaha is played for a wide variety of limits. What all of these limits have in common is that they adhere to the same betting structure, which is a 1:2 betting ratio. The bets before the flop and on the flop will be exactly one small bet (the lower betting tier), and the bets on the turn and river will be exactly one big bet (the higher betting tier — twice the small bet).

The most common limits for the small and big bets are (in $) 1-2, 2-4, 3-6, 4-8, 5-10, 10-20, 15-30, 20-40, 30-60, 60-120, 100-200, and 300-600. You must bet exactly the predetermined amount, which is why it's known as a structured game. You are not free to bet, for example, $4 or $5 in a $3-$6 game.

I've been asked why there are no $25-$50 and $50-$100 limit Omaha games. I've looked into it and what I learned was quite interesting. It seems that the casino poker rooms prefer not to host games that can be played exclusively with only green and red poker chips ($25 and $5 chips). Most poker players are reluctant to tip the dealer with a $5 chip, even if it's the smallest denomination chip used in the game. The poker room keeps white ($1) chips in play in all of its games so that the players will be more inclined to tip the dealers when they win a hand.

Another betting structure that's common at lower limits is called spread limit. A spread limit betting structure gives you more freedom—it allows you to bet any amount you choose at any time, as long as that amount is within the preset minimum and maximum.

The most common spread limit is $1-$5, meaning that you can bet any amount from $1 to $5. As in all other poker games, a raise must be at least the amount of the previous bet. There are a few significant differences between playing strategy and tactics in a spread limit game and in a structured game. We'll cover those in a later chapter.

Another popular betting structure is called $1-$4-$8-$8 limit. It's really a form of spread limit with some structure: you can bet from $1 to $4 before and after the flop and from $1 to $8 on the turn and the river.

Number of Players

Omaha can be played with as few as two and as many as eleven players. People generally look for tables with nine players, and many Las Vegas poker rooms play ten-handed. I believe that the best number of players to have at the table is eight or nine; I'll explain why later in the book.

HOW TO PLAY OMAHA

High (or Low) Hand Wins

Omaha can be played for high hand, for low hand, or for both high and low hand in the same game. Standard high hand wins. The lowest possible hand is a **wheel**, or a **bicycle**. Straights and flushes do not count against the low hand. There are no wild cards. Remember, the final poker hand is made up of exactly five cards.

The Two Card Rule

The key distinguishing feature of Omaha is the fact that you must use exactly two cards from your hand to make your poker hand. You cannot use only one card or three cards. This rule usually causes some confusion and results in misread hands among beginners, (and if the whole truth be known, among seasoned players as well). If there are four spades on the board, and you're holding the A♠, you don't have a flush (as you would in hold 'em). You'd also need another spade in your hand so that you'd be using exactly two cards in your hand and three cards on the board.

Since the rule is tricky, let's look at a few more examples. If there's a three-of-a-kind on the board, you don't have a full house unless you have a pair in your hand. For example, if the board is 5♠6♣6♥6♦J♦ and your hand is 5♦J♥Q♥A♦, you don't have a full house, even though you would in hold 'em. A jack or a 5 is only one card, and you must play two cards out of your hand. You need to be holding a pocket pair to make a full house when there are trips on the board.

Similarly, you do not have a full house when there are two pair on the board and you have one of those cards. If the board is 3♦3♣6♥J♦J♠ and you again have 5♦J♥Q♥A♦, the best hand you can make is three jacks with an ace kicker.

A player who has both a high and a low hand may use any combination of his cards that he chooses, as long as he uses exactly two cards from his hand to make each poker hand. Said another way, this means that he can use any two cards in his hand to make a high hand, and then he can use any two cards in his hand to make his low hand. They do not have to be the same cards for both hands, although they could be. For example, a player who holds A♦4♦J♥Q♥ with a board of 2♥3♣8♣9♠T♦ can use his A♦4♦ to make his low hand, and he can use his J♥Q♥ to make a straight.

Small Blind and Big Blind

Blinds are players who are forced to put money in the pot before the cards are dealt. The casino uses blinds to force action from the first two players to the left of the dealer. The **big blind** is always the same amount as the small bet and the **small blind** is one-half of the big blind. For example, the blinds in a $4-$8 game would be $2 in the small blind and $4 in the big blind. An exception is a $1-$4-$8-$8 limit game, in which the big blind is $2 and the small blind is $1.

In a game where the small blind can't be exactly half of the big blind, it's usually rounded down. For example, the blinds in a $3-$6 game should be $3 and $1.50 but, since a half-dollar is not a betting denomination, the blinds are $3 and $1. The same principle applies in a $15-$30 game where the blinds should be $15 and $7.50. The small blind is rounded down, so the blinds are $15 and $5, or three red chips and one red chip. Did you notice that a $3-$6 game is the same as a $15-$30 game, with only the color of the chips being different?

The purpose of having two blinds is to create a situation where two of the players will have random hands, since they put their money in the pot before seeing their hands, and other players will have voluntarily entered the pot after looking at their hands. This mix of totally random hands and the hands that the other players wish to play against them is designed to create a contest for the pot when the flop comes. Because of the two blind feature of the game, there is no ante in Omaha, as there is in stud or draw poker.

Play of the Game

Each player is dealt four cards face down. These cards are called the pocket cards. Do not show these cards to any other player, since they constitute your entire private hand.

Remember that the blinds have to put their bets in the pot before the deal. The play now starts with the player to the immediate left of the big blind and moves clockwise. Each player has three options. He can **fold** (**muck** his hand), call (keep his hand and put the correct amount of money in the pot), or raise (increase the bet by at least as much as the previous bet).

If no one has raised by the time the action comes back to the small blind, he can either fold, call (put in enough money to make up the difference between his bet and the big blind's bet), or raise at least the amount of the big blind. For example, in a $1-$4-$8-$8 game where the big blind is $2, a raise of $1 is not permitted. All raises in poker must be for at least the amount of the previous bet.

In a structured game, the raise must be exactly the small-tiered amount. Since the blinds had to put their money in the pot before they saw their hands, they also have the option of raising themselves.

If no one has raised by the time the action gets back around to the big blind, he then has the option to raise. The dealer will ask him, "Option?" and the big blind has to answer with either "Check" ("I bet nothing more") or "I raise."

The Flop

After this first betting round is completed, the dealer burns the top card (removes it from play), and turns the next three cards face up on the board. This is the **flop**. There is a second round of betting, beginning with the small blind or the first player in the hand after the small blind if he's out. This round is played with a small bet and three raise limit. Players may check (bet nothing) and pass on to the next player until someone bets.

HOW TO PLAY OMAHA

Once a bet is made, however, players must either call the bet, raise, or fold and go out of play for the remainder of the hand. Checking is no longer an option once a bet is made. This rule holds true for all rounds of play. Some poker rooms have a four raise or even a five raise limit, so it's wise to know the limits before you start playing.

The Turn

After the second betting round, the dealer burns another card, and then turns the next card face up on the table. This fourth community card is called the **turn**. A third round of betting among the remaining players follows, only this time you can bet from $1 to $8 in the $1-$4-$8-$8 game or the higher amount in the structured game. For example, in a $3-$6 game you must now bet or raise in $6 increments.

The River

After the action is completed on the turn, the dealer again burns the top card. He now turns a fifth, and final, card face up on the board. There is a final round of betting, called the **river**, which follows the same betting guidelines as the turn.

The Showdown

When all the action is completed, there is a **showdown**. All the active players who want to claim the pot turn their hands face up. Using his pocket cards and the five cards on the board, each player (with the dealer) determines his best poker hand. High hand wins half of the pot and, if there is a qualifying low hand, the other half of the pot is awarded to the low hand. In the event that two or more players have identical hands, they split their half of the pot among themselves. If there is no qualifying low hand, the high hand wins the entire pot.

The dealer **button** then moves one player to the left, marking the new dealer's position. The blinds are posted by the next two players, and the game begins all over again.

Last Thought on Dealing

The only difference between dealing Texas hold 'em and dealing Omaha is that after dealing everyone two cards, the dealer then continues to deal until everyone has four cards. That's not a big difference in how the game is dealt, but what results from the addition of those two extra cards are the contents of the rest of this book.

3

HOW OMAHA DIFFERS FROM TEXAS HOLD 'EM

The addition of two extra cards to a hold 'em hand to create an Omaha hand has an incredible effect on how the game is played. The strategies and tactics you use to play hold 'em apply in a completely different way when you're playing Omaha. Some of them hardly apply at all. The stipulation that you must play exactly two of those cards from your hand further complicates the game and makes it more interesting. If you then play the game for hi-low split, you've added another dimension, and it requires you to do a lot more thinking during the play of a hand. In summary, there's a lot more going on during the play of an Omaha hand than there is during the play of a hold 'em hand.

Starting with some general observations and then working toward the specific details, here's a list of ways in which Omaha differs from Texas hold 'em:

1. Omaha is played for higher limits. Omaha is usually played for hi-low split, which means that players will often win one-half of a pot instead of the whole pot. Because people don't want to win much less than they would at hold 'em, the limits are usually doubled, so that what is one-half of an Omaha pot is approximately equal to a whole hold 'em pot. A $6-$12 hi-low Omaha game is the equivalent of a $3-$6 hold 'em game. Do not be intimidated by the higher stakes; they aren't really higher stakes, because you'll be getting half a pot twice as often.

2. Bankroll requirements are higher. Not only do you actually need more money to make that higher buy-in, the swings in Omaha are also more frequent and volatile than they are in hold 'em. Omaha attracts action-oriented players. Players who like to do a lot of betting and raising while drawing to their hands will make it more expensive for you to play your hands. If you miss a few draws and make a few second-best hands without winning a pot here and there, you could be investing a lot of money in one playing session. To survive these setbacks, you need to have a bigger cash reserve than you would in hold 'em.

3. Kill games are much more common. A **kill game** is a game in which the betting limits are increased (usually doubled) for the next hand only. Sometimes, a poker room manager will not want to offer a limit that is twice that of the hold 'em game. It may be because you're in a small room without the clientele needed to support the bigger game, or it may be due to player preference. Recognizing that a good Omaha hi-low game should be played at higher stakes than the hold 'em game, the manager will then compromise by offering Omaha hi-low with a kill. About two-thirds of the games will be played at the lower limit, and one-third will be played at the higher limit.

In my opinion, the best Omaha and hold 'em games with a kill in the country are at the Vee Quiva Casino in Phoenix, Arizona. The poker room management is the best anywhere, the games are nine-handed, you can eat your meal at the table, the service is excellent, the dealers are superb, and the other players are...well, they make a lot of mistakes and they have a lot of money (nothing personal, guys). My big bet per hour win rate there looks like a misprint in my record books.

4. Betting structure is sometimes different. Because Omaha attracts players who like to play most hands, and because it is correct to call more often after the flop, the pots get big early in the play of a hand. Sometimes, an Omaha pot will be as big before the flop as a hold 'em pot is at the river. Because pots grow so quickly, each succeeding bet that goes into the pot on the flop and later rounds is a smaller and smaller percentage of the pot. Everyone will almost always have the right odds to keep drawing. Even hands that have only two outs will have the correct odds to pay to draw, which is almost unheard of in hold 'em.

The bets double after the flop in flop games in recognition of the fact that players with made hands have a right to bet to protect themselves against players with drawing hands. In hold 'em, the drawing hands will often correctly fold rather than chase their draws. Not so in Omaha! Because the Omaha pot is so big, it would be wrong for them to fold. To remedy this situation, some Omaha games are played with a 1:2:3:4 betting ratio, or even a 1:2:4:4 ratio.

In a multiple of a 1:2:3:4 game, for example, you can bet $3 before the flop, $6 on the flop, $9 on the turn, and $12 on the river.

These multi-tiered betting limits work very well and make for a great game. Don't forget that when you play in a public poker room, *you are the customer.* If you're playing an Omaha game with a traditional 1:2 betting ratio and the bad players are always drawing out on you, then you should talk to the manager about changing the betting structure to the one I just described. It can only help you, and you will like it.

5. Omaha hi-low has the lowest fluctuation. A lot of bad players like to play Omaha because it's an action game. They can always find a hand to play. After all, you can make six separate hold 'em hands from one Omaha hand. When all is said and done, these players are the biggest losers. They have the biggest swings in their bankrolls, and if you're not careful, they can take you down with them.

For the player who has the right skills and the determination to put those skills to work, however, Omaha hi-low split has the lowest fluctuation of any poker game commonly played. In other words, among similarly (highly) skilled hold 'em, Omaha, stud, and draw players who have similar bankrolls and play for similar stakes, it is the Omaha player who will be most assured of not losing his bankroll. He'll have the best chance of being a winner in the long run. The purpose of this book is to turn you into that Omaha player.

6. Omaha is better for you when playing against bad players. An Omaha player and a hold 'em player who are equally bad at the game will both be losers in the long run, no matter which game they play. It's more profitable for you to play against the bad Omaha player. In addition to making the same mistakes as the hold 'em player, he will be putting a lot more money in action when he makes those mistakes. Having more money in the pots that you win obviously means bigger profits for you.

In a hold 'em game, three or four players might typically see the flop. There will be an occasional pre-flop raise, and the action will usually be bet-call or check-call to the river. Not so in an Omaha game. In Omaha, almost everyone will see the flop. Unless low is impossible, almost everyone will also then see the turn and the river cards (while raising and re-raising like crazy along the way). Players who would never play this way in hold 'em play this way all of the time in Omaha. The Omaha game is where you want to be.

7. Omaha is more profitable. If you understand everything you've read to this point, that's a logical conclusion. Between two similarly skilled Omaha and hold 'em players, the Omaha player will have won more money at the end of every year than the hold 'em player has won. The pots are bigger, which in turn translates into more big bets won per hour. And that's what it's really all about.

8. Superior players are handicapped. As you will see, there are a lot of skills that are required for hold 'em that are not as important for Omaha. Players who are very good because they possess those skills cannot use them against you in an Omaha game. This levels the playing field a little, and the difference in the skill levels of the best and worst players is therefore less pronounced than it is in hold 'em.

Imagine you have a poker IQ of 110 points, and the Albert Einstein of poker takes a seat in your Omaha game (he's toting a poker IQ of 210 points). Intimidated? Don't be. Ninety of his poker IQ points represent knowledge that the structure and nature of Omaha prevent him from using against you. 210 minus ninety equals 120. Now, how much better is he than you? Not much.

I'm convinced that once you achieve a certain level of competence in this game, you can confidently hold your own against any professional player in a limit Omaha game. And guess what? The professional players know that, too. That's why they prefer to play very high limit, pot limit, and no limit — but that's another subject.

9. Omaha hand values are different. Top pair with top kicker and top two pair are the bread-and-butter hands of hold 'em. In that game, these hands, along with an uncalled bet on the river, are what wins the pot more than any other hands. If these were the hands I held on the river in Omaha, however, I wouldn't even call a bet.

Because holding four cards allows you to make six different two-card hold 'em hands, and you might be playing against eight opponents, playing nine-handed Omaha is almost the same as playing in a 54-handed hold 'em game! You'll have to have the nuts almost every time to win the pot. Hand values have to be adjusted upward — dramatically.

It's no longer a question of "How likely is it that my opponent has the nuts?" When you're looking at fifty-four different hands out there against you, it's really a question of "How could anyone not have the nuts?" In Omaha, there's always someone who has the current nuts, and there's always someone drawing to an even better hand. If that player's not you…

10. Omaha is more fun to play. And that's not because you have to play poorly to have fun. It's because, given six possible hands to play, you will get a good hand and/or a good draw on the flop more often that you would if you were playing just one hand. You will have more outs than you would in the same situation in hold 'em. Plus, the pot will be bigger, so it will be correct to call in Omaha where it would be correct to fold in hold 'em. The structure of the game allows you to correctly play more hands, see more flops, call more bets and raises, chase more draws, put more of your chips in action, and win bigger pots. And that's fun.

11. Omaha offers more outs. Your **outs** are the number of cards that will help your hand. If you're playing hi-low, and you're playing correctly, your hand will usually give you more than one way to win. You could be drawing to a straight and a flush while having a good low draw working. If you also flopped a set, you'd also be drawing to a full house. Whenever you have nine cards of one suit, eight cards to make a straight, sixteen cards to make a low, and ten cards to pair the board — and you get two draws at it — you have outs! How long do you have to play hold 'em to get all of those draws?

12. Pot odds are better. The term **pot odds** refers to the ratio of the amount of money in the pot to the amount of money that it costs to call a bet. If you have a straight- or a flush-draw in a hold 'em game, you will usually get the right odds to draw to the hand often enough to show a profit in that situation. The same thing will happen in Omaha, only those extra bets giving you the odds you need will be in the pot earlier in the hand than they would be in the hold 'em game. You will often know after seeing the flop that you hold a through ticket, just because the pot is already so big.

13. Implied odds are better. The phrase "implied odds" means the ratio of the amount of money you think you will win if you make your hand to the amount of money you must call now to keep playing the hand. "I don't have the right odds to call with this hand, but, if I call and make my draw, I can raise, and those extra bets will make up for the bets that I need that aren't in the pot right now. I can get them in the pot after I make the hand." If this is what you're thinking, then you're thinking about implied odds. The fact that you can be sure more players will call more bets in Omaha means that you will have the implied odds you need to play your drawing hands.

There's another source of implied odds that's overlooked in Omaha hi-low — players who are drawing to low hands will not always qualify for low. If you're playing for high, you will often scoop a pot when the low doesn't get there. They will put money in the pot and then be eliminated from the competition by the rules of the game. Whenever you're playing for high and low hasn't gotten there yet, you have additional implied odds.

14. The small blind almost always plays. Due to the larger than average number of players who will call before the flop, the fact that he can make six hold 'em hands with his Omaha hand, and the fact that he can get in for a partial bet, the small blind rarely folds in Omaha. Remember, he's not always playing poorly. It's just that given the pot odds he's getting, it would be wrong for him to fold most hands.

15. Seat selection is less important. It's not unimportant, just less important. In poker, you want players with certain characteristics to sit on your immediate right or left, depending on what those characteristics are. Because everyone has so many hands to draw to, the pot is so big, everyone has so many outs, and everyone needs to see the river card, a player can't make a move on the pot. Generally, in Omaha, the correct play is to play in a straightforward manner. Do the obvious thing, and hope you win the pot.

16. Incorrect early position play is more costly. If you're in early position, and you have to call a raise before the flop, your natural tendency will be to call when you should usually fold. Because you can see so many possibilities in your hand, and because the pot is already so big, you will misjudge the value of your hand. The pre-flop raise usually means that the raiser is drawing to the nuts, and the fact is: you can't win this hand even if you're getting 1,000,000:1 odds. The point is that if you were holding a similarly weak hand in the same position in a hold 'em game, you'd quickly muck the hand. Omaha is a seductive game.

17. Holding a dominated hand is less of a problem. A **dominated hand** is a hand that nearly always loses when competing against another particular hand. In hold 'em, a dominated hand is typically a 4:1 underdog. That's 80%-20%. In Omaha, the worst hand is no worse than a 3:2 underdog. That's 60%-40%. Your hand depends on what comes on the flop and on how many outs you have to make your hand, and that means that you're not penalized as much for playing a bad hand in Omaha as you are in hold 'em. *But don't be mislead by that statement.* The truth is that you'll still lose in the long run if you consistently play bad hands, even if some of those bad hands aren't as bad as others.

Don't lose sight of the big picture. Playing a bad hand in hold 'em is like drowning in forty feet of water. Playing a bad hand in Omaha is like drowning in only twenty feet of water. You really don't want to do either.

18. Drawing dead is more costly. Because you'll be calling more bets and raises, you'll be putting more money into the pot. Obviously, this means that you'll be investing a lot of money in losing hands. Why would you do that? You do it because you don't recognize that you may be drawing dead. With six different hands to play, you delude yourself into believing that one of them will come through for you. Unfortunately, the only way to learn how to avoid drawing dead is through experience.

On the other hand, the good news is that drawing dead is relatively common in an Omaha game. Hopefully, for every pot that you lose because you're drawing dead, the other players will draw dead against you many more times. Once you learn how to avoid drawing dead, a substantial part of your profits will come from the other players who don't play or draw to the nuts.

19. Omaha jackpots are easier to hit. In hold 'em, it takes about 12,500 hands to hit a jackpot. In Omaha, hitting a jackpot is about four times easier. Hold 'em players have only one hand to play at a time, while Omaha players have six hands to play all at once. So why isn't it six times easier to hit instead of four? Because you cannot make a qualifying **bad beat** hand with 2s and 3s, and some jackpots require that four-of-a-kind or better be the bad beat hand.

20. Raising is less effective. There are five reasons to raise:

1. To eliminate players
2. To get a free card
3. To gain information
4. To get value from your hand
5. To bluff or semi-bluff

When you realize that every player has six hold 'em hands, that players can play for high or low, that they're getting the right odds to play, that they know the pot is going to be big, and that they're going to see the river card no matter what, you can see that this takes away some of your options. You may not be able to accomplish some of your goals of raising when playing against them.

Let's see how effective raising is in an Omaha game when we re-evaluate each reason to raise in light of what I've just told you about Omaha:

1. Whom do you think you're going to eliminate by raising, especially before the flop? Players with genuinely garbage hands were going to fold anyway. Players who want to see the flop know that the flop could be anything, and with six hands to play they will get some piece of it.

Raising *on* the flop to eliminate players also doesn't work very well. Anyone who picked up a completed hand, a straight- or flush-draw, a four-card low, two pair, or a set has a through ticket. The only players who will fold when you raise on the flop are the ones who completely missed the flop or who flopped only one pair and no other hand or draw. And they were going to fold for one bet anyway!

2. Raising on the flop to get everyone to check to you on the turn (that's how you get the free card) doesn't work either. There are so many hands out there against you that some of them are hands that must be bet for value. For this play to work, every single player in the game had to have flopped only draws to straights or flushes or weak pairs, and that just doesn't happen.

3. Raising to get information doesn't help much because the response you get will be difficult to interpret. Players who call your raise are telling you...what? They have made hands? They're on draws to the nuts? They *have* the nuts? They're on low draws? With so many possible hands, the answer is yes to everything. So how did the raise help you? If you raise and are re-raised, then you know the re-raiser has the nuts, and usually with a draw to an even better hand. Someone always has the nuts and is drawing to a better nut hand in Omaha. You know that. So how did the raise help you? Not much.

4. Raising to get value from your hand means you are building a pot you expect to win. In my opinion, this is by far the best reason to raise in Omaha. For the most part, it should be the only reason to raise in Omaha.

5. Raising to bluff will work in Omaha in only one very specific, infrequent, narrowly defined situation. Before

you read further, take a minute to see if you can figure out which situation I mean.

Got it yet? Let's say you've played to the river and there's just you and one opponent left in the hand. He must act first. He bets, and *you know he's bluffing.* (Sometimes a player will be on a big draw, miss on the turn and river, and be left with no poker hand to speak of.) In this case, you can raise him with nothing, and he will not call. This situation occurs once in a blue moon. (A blue moon is the second full moon in a calendar month — it occurs about once every thirteen months.)

Semi-bluffing is defined as betting with a hand that, if called, probably isn't the best hand at the moment, but has a chance to improve with more cards to come. Raising to semi-bluff doesn't work well because of the same reasons that raising to get a free card doesn't work. Someone will always have a hand that he needs to protect by betting for value.

Knowing when to raise, why to raise, and sometimes who to raise is one of the most powerful tools that the expert player has in his arsenal of weapons to use against you. It's what makes him a professional. However, when he takes a seat in your Omaha game he must, like the gunslingers of yesteryear, check his weapons at the door. This is exactly what I was getting at with the poker IQ analogy in #8, earlier. An expert has this knowledge, but, because of the nature of the game, he can't use it against you. It's almost as if he didn't have that knowledge to begin with.

21. Bluffing is a smaller part of the game. I'm talking about betting as a bluff, not raising as a bluff. If you have a totally busted hand (one with no chance of winning on its own) and have to bluff at the pot to have any chance to win it, you're very likely to be called in an Omaha game. Again, when everyone has six hands, someone will have something with which to call you. This rule is especially true on the river, when there are five more cards to add to everyone's hand.

Generally, to **bluff** means to bet with a hand that you're sure will lose if called. A pure bluff opportunity does arise infrequently on the river in Omaha. It's when the flop presents two low cards (and/or two flush cards) and the low (and/or flush) doesn't get there on the turn or the river. If you know your opponents and they respect you, you can bluff at this pot often enough to show a profit in the long run. They'll give you credit for the nut set (or best hand — which is so easy to have in this game), and they'll throw away everything between ace-high and bottom set. They'll "know" that you were waiting for the straight and flush draws to miss before betting your hand for value.

Don't ever, ever, *ever* let anyone know if you've just won a pot by bluffing in Omaha. All Omaha players know that someone "always" has a hand at the river and that bluffing is normally out of the question. Bluff opportunities *do* arise, however rarely, and they represent a very profitable situation for the knowledgeable player. Pots won by bluffing add significantly to your Big Bets Won Per Hour statistic.

Since the pots are usually big, and it takes only one call to snap off a bluff attempt, you do not want to acquire a reputation as a frequent bluffer in this game. If you do, you will never again win a pot by bluffing. In hold 'em, there are a lot of good reasons why you'd want to advertise a successful bluff. Not one of those reasons applies to Omaha. Save advertising for the hold 'em game.

22. Check-raising is less effective. To **check-raise** means not to bet initially on a round, and then to raise when the action returns to you. There are two reasons to check-raise: to force players to call two or more bets cold (at once) and to trap players for an extra bet after they've already called one bet in that round. Check-raising is usually *not* a good play in Omaha. Why?

1. It's usually a better strategy to bet to get immediate value from your hand.
2. You need to make the drawing hands pay.
3. You can't always count on someone betting for you if you check.
4. As the pot gets bigger, you should play your hand in the way that maximizes your chances of winning the pot, even if it makes you feel like you might be giving your hand away. This is a very important principle of poker theory, and it almost always means bet and raise instead of check and slow-play.

Revealing the strength of your hand in Omaha is not as detrimental to your cause as it would be in hold 'em, draw, or stud. In Omaha, everyone already knows that you have (or should have) the nuts with a draw to an even better hand. There's no secret here. Other players will know the type of hand you're playing, even if they don't know the exact cards you're holding. A quick reading of the board will tell them the contents of your hand.

23. Slow-playing is usually incorrect. To **slow-play** means to play your hand in a much weaker manner than its strength would usually call for in order to disguise your strength for a future betting round. You should understand by now why you can't play your strong hand in a weak manner, why you can't check when you should be betting, and why you can't give free cards if you have a good hand. There is one instance, however, when it is okay to slow-play. Take a minute to see if you can figure out when I mean.

Got it yet? It's when your hand is insured. How does your hand get to be insured? When you make four-of-a-kind or better using two of your pocket cards — thereby qualifying for the jackpot if you lose the hand. *Now* you can check and slow-play and hope that you're giving someone a better chance to draw out on you.

24. There's less guessing in Omaha. Since everyone is trying to make the nuts or already has the nuts, you know your opponents are not bluffing. They expect to be called when they bet, and all you have to do is look at the board to know what they have. The player betting first almost always has exactly what he's supposed to have. You know it, and he knows that you know it. For that reason, you can correctly give him credit for having the hand he's representing. You don't have to guess.

25. You're going to have to fold better hands. This is a hard one. Hold 'em players are accustomed to trying to make top sets, straights, and flushes so they can win big pots with those hands. They have a hard time throwing those hands away on the river in Omaha. These hands are high on the poker hand scale, and, statistically speaking, they are difficult to make.

Here's where you have to make a big adjustment for hand values. As you know by now, there are many more hands playing against you in Omaha than there are in hold 'em.

I perform a mental exercise that helps me keep this aspect of the game in proper perspective. It works well for me, and it adds to my hourly win rate. I'd like to share it with you:

Imagine you are playing in a ten-handed Omaha game. Each of the nine other players can make six hold 'em hands with his one Omaha hand. This makes a total of fifty-four hands that you're playing against. Now imagine that instead of nine players each holding six hands there are fifty-four players (!) holding each one of those hands. Now you're going to ask all of those players to stand up. In order for you to win this hand, you need to get all of them seated again. Here goes.

When the flop comes, you say, "Everyone who was playing

for low and missed, sit down. Everyone who was trying to make a small set, sit down. Everyone who was trying to make a flush and missed or can't draw, sit down. Everyone who was trying to make a straight and got a bad flop, sit down." Perhaps half of your opponents are now seated.

When the turn card comes, go through the same process, and that should eliminate a few more players. When the river card comes, you say, "Everyone who does not have the nuts or the near nuts sit down."

The point of this exercise is that you must realize that there will be someone left standing *almost every time*. The flop will not always eliminate everyone playing against you. I hope this trick helps you realize that.

26. Doubt is good in Omaha. In hold 'em, if a sole opponent bets into you on the river and you genuinely don't know what to do, more often than not, you will have to lean toward calling. The pot will be relatively big by then, and besides, it's so easy for one player to be bluffing in this spot in hold 'em. In Omaha, that same decision on the river is a lot easier to make. If you're really undecided, it means that *your* hand is not that good. You can fold better hands and have more confidence that you're doing the right thing in Omaha than you would have in hold 'em. You will be bluffed out of the pot less often in Omaha because the nature of the game requires the bettor to attempt a bluff less often.

27. There are more protected pots in Omaha. A protected pot is one that has a huge number of bets in it compared to the average size of other pots. It's a pot that is so big that when there is a bet at the river, someone who would not otherwise call *will* call just because of the pot size and the odds he's getting. You usually must have to have the nuts on the river, or you might have only a 2% chance of bluffing. If you're playing for a protected pot, though, you're really going to have the nuts, and you'll have almost no chance of bluffing.

28. Hand selection is the key Omaha skill. If you're an experienced hold 'em player and you understand the theory, strategy, and tactics of poker, then you have quite a repertoire of skills available to you in your poker arsenal. You know that there are about ten major skills that constitute 90% of your skill at hold 'em, and you know that there are dozens of minor skills that make up the other 10% of your skill at the game. If you have a weakness in any one of those ten major skills, then you'll have a big leak in your hold 'em game.

Omaha is completely different. Skill at hand selection is the one major skill that constitutes 90% of your skill at this game. All of the other skills are minor and make up the other 10% of your skill at the game. The nature of the game is what makes skill at hand selection so important in Omaha. Deciding whether to call to see the flop is the most important decision you'll make in Omaha. If you can't make it correctly, then, ultimately nothing else matters.

If you get nothing else out of this book (or if you don't even read another page), at the very least, you need to understand that skill at hand selection is the one and only thing that you need to master at Omaha (assuming you're already an experienced hold 'em player). If you don't play the right hands from the beginning, then nothing else matters.

Proper hand selection is the secret of Omaha. Let me tell you how skill at hand selection affects me personally. When I play Omaha and I use my best judgment and expertise when choosing which hands to play, my stack of chips grows slowly and steadily. When I get ahead and I decide to play more (weaker) hands in an effort to win more pots, my stack of chips shrinks slowly and steadily. When I see my chips disappearing and tighten up my starting hand requirements, the stack again grows slowly and steadily. I can literally control the number of poker chips I have in front of me by changing my starting hand requirements.

In Omaha, you must have the best possible high or low hand at the river to win the pot. No amount of skill at poker will win the hand for you if your cards can't beat your opponents' because you didn't select the right hand to play from the beginning.

29. Patience is the key attribute. Hand selection is the key skill. That means you are going to be selective and play only hands that meet certain predetermined criteria. You won't be playing a lot of hands, and that in turn makes patience the best attribute to have. Since it takes more time to deal and play a hand of Omaha than a hand of hold 'em, fewer Omaha hands are dealt per hour than hold 'em hands. That means you'll be sitting out a lot. You won't be in action like everyone else around you. You will be tempted to play a hand out of boredom or because you can see possibilities in it.

Learn to resist that temptation. Tell yourself that you're passing hands that you know other bad players would be calling with. Follow the action on a bad hand, and calculate how much money you saved by not playing it. Congratulate yourself. Use the time to watch the other players. Practice your hand reading skills. Practice your ability to read tells. Practice figuring out what the nut low is, which is always a bit tricky to do. You can go to the bathroom, although I never go to the bathroom when playing Omaha, because I might miss a $300 pot and there's nothing in the bathroom worth $300. The point is, do anything you have to do to keep from playing inferior starting hands.

30. Suited aces are worth a lot more than unsuited ones. In hold 'em, you can have A X (where "X" denotes any random card) unsuited and win good-sized pots quite often with it. In Omaha, all four of your cards have to work together for you to be a consistent winner. That means if you have an ace in your hand, it is a big plus if you have another card of that suit. This allows you to draw to a big hand (the flush) and then have the nuts when you make it. If three cards of your suit are on the board and you have the ace, you have a hand that you can use to make the other players call raises if they're trying to draw out on you.

31. Ace-little is worth a lot more. An ace with a small, unsuited card in hold 'em is a trap hand. When playing for low in Omaha, A 2, A 3, A 4, and A 5 can make the nuts for you. It helps if you have another low card to go with this hand.

32. Middle cards are more costly. Since Omaha is a hi-low game, you must have the very best high cards and the very best low cards to win. All of the cards that you're using to make your hand must be either the nut low or the nut high cards (or both). There's no such game as Omaha middle, although it seems that a lot of players like to play it anyway. Computer analysis has revealed that the 7, 8, and 9 are the most costly cards to have in your hand if you're playing hi-low split (duh!) Pocket 7s, 8s, and 9s, along with 8 7s ("s" in this context stands for "suited,") 98s, and 97s, can be very good hold 'em hands, but if you never played another Omaha hand with a 7, 8, or 9 in it for the rest of your poker playing life, you'd be adding to your win rate and your overall amount of money won while reducing the fluctuations in your bankroll.

33. Beware of A A X X. In hold 'em, it's automatic to raise before the flop with pocket aces. Not so in Omaha. A low flop in hold 'em helps your hand, while a low flop in Omaha hurts your hand because it gives all the low pairs and draws a hand that beats you.

For this reason, most Omaha players prefer to limp in with A A X X and see the flop. In Omaha, it often happens that the board is something like A♠5♣9♥J♦9♣ and someone who never raised at any time surprises you by showing you pocket aces to make the full house.

34. Kickers are more important. Your **kicker** is the highest card in your hand that does not help make a straight, flush, or full house. If you have A♥J♥ in hold 'em and you flop another ace against a sole opponent who also holds an ace, your chances of winning the hand are pretty good, because he has only one other card with which to beat your kicker. In Omaha, he has three other cards in his hand to give him a chance to beat your kicker. Enough said.

35. Late position is worth less. The benefits of being in late position in hold 'em just don't apply in Omaha. You can't raise to steal the blinds, and you can't raise to isolate the big blind. You can't raise to get information, to eliminate anyone, to get free cards, or to vary your play. You *can* raise in late position to get value from your hand, and you should do so when you have one of the premium starting hands, such as a potential nut-nut scoop hand. A♦A♥2♦K♥ is an excellent example of a late position pre-flop raising hand.

36. High cards are worth less. Why? Because players who are playing for low can end up with high-ranking poker hands. You can't play low cards in hold 'em trying to make a straight. You'll miss your straight draw too often, and you will sometimes lose to a higher hand when you do make the straight. It's just not profitable. In Omaha, however, if you play low cards, get a straight draw, and miss, you can still get half of the pot by making a low hand, which is impossible in hold 'em. Players who are playing for low are freerolling for high. Players who are playing for high can never win the low pot.

37. Bicycles are more likely. A **bicycle**, also called a **wheel**, is a 5-high straight: 5 4 3 2 A. The nut low hand is a bicycle. Everyone playing for low will have two, three, or four low cards in his hand. If the flop helps his low draw (chance to hold four low cards and need only one more for a completed low hand), someone will usually end up with that perfect low hand. Someone could also make 2 3 4 5 6 for a 6-high straight or 3 4 5 6 7 for a 7-high straight. If you're playing for high and you make two big pair, you're going to lose a hand at Omaha that you would not have lost at hold 'em. In Omaha, low draws can end up with high hands.

38. Your poker hand goal is different. In hold 'em, you're usually trying to make top pair with top kicker or possibly top two pair to win the pot. In Omaha, these hands will hardly ever win the pot. Often, the only way you can win with them is if everyone checks on the river. You normally can't expect to call a bet on the river and actually have the best hand.

Your real objective in Omaha (high) is to make one of three completed hands: a straight, a flush, or a full house. This requirement puts you in a position where you have the nuts if you make the hand, and it helps keep you from playing inferior starting hands. Four-of-a-kind and a straight-flush are also completed hands, but they are bonus hands that you will make only occasionally as a result of trying to make a flush or full house. These hands are not your primary goal in each hand you play.

TIP: Many good Omaha players do not always play every high hand where the logical made hand can be only a straight. If I hold 9♠J♣Q♥A♦ in an early position, or if I have to call pre-flop raises with that hand, I will usually not play the hand. I know that I can make only one hand with it, and I have no possibility of drawing to a higher hand after that. Actually, the worst thing that can happen with this hand is to make the straight on the flop, because every card that comes on the turn and river gives everyone a chance to beat you. This is not a bad hand, however. I would play it in late position. It's just that it would be a lot better if it had another diamond to give you the additional draw that you need for insurance.

39. Small sets are more dangerous. If you hold 2♥5♣7♠7♦ and you get another 7 on the flop, you have a very vulnerable hand. Any overcard on the turn or river could give someone a higher set, simply because so many of the players will be holding pocket pairs in their hands. Small sets usually win small pots and lose big ones. There are exceptions, but you must still play your small sets very carefully. Don't get attached to them.

40. Cold calling is more correct. If you have a draw in hold 'em and you have to call two or more bets cold, you will often have to fold your hand because you won't have the right odds to draw. The pot will be small in relation to the amount of money you'd have to call, and you will rarely have more than eight or nine outs. Not so in Omaha. The pot will usually have bets from most players in the game, and you will usually have twelve to twenty-four outs. This makes it correct to cold call. Even with the raise, you still have the right odds to call.

41. Backdoor draws are more common. A **backdoor** draw is a draw to a hand that you originally weren't trying to get. If you're trying to make one type of hand in hold 'em and the turn and river cards give you a chance to make another type of hand, you usually won't be able to make that second type of hand because you won't have enough cards to go around.

Let's say you hold A♣6♣, and the flop is 3♣7♣T♥. You have a good flush draw. If the turn is the J♠ and the river is the K♦, you could also make the nut straight — if you also happened to be holding a queen. In Omaha, it's much more likely that someone will be holding the two cards needed for a straight (an ace and a queen), because everyone has four cards instead of just two. It seems that in Omaha, no matter what comes on the turn or river, someone has it covered.

42. Threats are more real. When the flop is all one suit, it's very easy for one or more of eight or nine other players to be holding two cards of that suit. When there's a pair on the flop it's easy for anyone to be holding one of those cards to make trips — or even a full house. These flops are dangerous enough in hold 'em. The threat is more real in Omaha because almost all of the cards in the deck are in the hands of your opponents.

Assume you're in a ten-handed Omaha game. The flop is J♦J♥6♣, and you don't have a jack in your hand. With one burn card gone, four cards in your hand, and thirty-six (9x4) cards in the other players' hands, there are eleven cards left in the deck.

Q: What are the odds that both of the remaining jacks are still in the deck (and that one or both of them are not in someone's hand)?

A: About 35-1 against.

A good rule of thumb is: if the flop has paired and it didn't help you, then it has hurt you. There's no in between in this spot in Omaha.

43. Double flush draws are more likely. If the flop is 6♥Q♥8♣, then you're usually looking at a flush draw. If the turn card is another club, then you're usually looking at two flush draws. The pot odds, the four-card hand and the number of outs all conspire to make players holding two clubs stay to see the river card. With two flush draws on the board, almost half of the deck will make a flush for one of your opponents.

44. Three flush cards means a flush! Just like a pair on the flop means someone has trips, a flop with three cards of the same suit usually means someone has a flush. The good news is that these flushes won't always be the nuts. If someone holds A♣2♥3♦6♥ and the flop is 8♥J♥K♥, he has a flush. If he's a good player, though, he will probably check and fold. It's too easy for another player to be holding a higher flush, especially if that player is betting. Notice that if you flop a flush, another flush card on the turn or river doesn't necessarily help or hurt you unless a straight flush is possible.

45. Overcards are killers. An **overcard** is a card on the board that's higher than any of your hole cards. In Omaha, every card on the board represents the very real possibility that someone is using that card to make a set. If you have a low set and a card higher than your set comes, you no longer have the nuts. The chances are pretty good that the new card matches someone else's pocket pair. Even if it doesn't make someone a higher set, it does make a straight or a flush draw possible.

46. Free cards are killers. A **free card** is a card you receive on a betting round where there's no betting because everyone checks. There's not much difference between a free card and an overcard in Omaha. One is free, and the other costs very little in relation to the size of the final pot. The difference lies in knowing that it's bad to give your opponents a free card. Do the correct thing and make them pay for it, even if it's likely that the next card could be an overcard that hurts you. Attitude check: free cards are something that your opponents are supposed to give you — not something you give them.

47. A full house is not a big hand. In flop games, depending on the cards in your hand, the strength of your hand is situational and relative. A full house ranks high on the list of poker hands, but you must view it in light of the other cards on the board, the number of other players in the hand, and whether the game is hold 'em or Omaha. If, in hold 'em, you hold A♥A♦ against one player and the board is A♣J♥7♦5♠5♣, you have the virtual nuts. The other player must hold 5♥5♦ to beat you, and the odds against that are 1,325-1.

If the game is Omaha, though, you have a very different situation. Let's say you hold 5♦6♥7♣7♠ and the board is 7♥K♦K♥A♣A♠. Including you, there are eight players in the hand. You still have a full house, but you have no strength due to the other cards on the board and the number of players (combined cards) playing against you. It's just too easy for someone to be holding AA, KK, AK, A7 or K7 and beat you. In fact, if someone bets, what could he possibly have that you can beat? Learn to be more alert when you make a full house, and slow down when you must.

48. Freerolling is much more common. Freerolling means having the nuts *and* a draw to a better hand when there are still more cards to come. It's more common in Omaha — as you can see by now, that's just the nature of the game. You shouldn't be trying to make just one hand anyway. (The only exception to that rule is if you have four wheel cards in your hand with no flush possibilities.) With five cards on the board and four more in your hand, you can see how easy it is to make a straight on your way to making a flush or a flush on your way to making a full house. Don't forget that players with low hands are freerolling for high. They could possibly make a low straight or perhaps even a backdoor flush.

49. Hand reading skills are less important. The three main tools that help you read other players' hands — position, psychology and statistics — are of less use to you in an Omaha game. Since all players have six possible hands, you can never be sure exactly which one to put a player on early in the hand. You will, however, be able to tell if he's going high or low, especially if there are only high or low cards on the flop and he keeps playing.

Since an Omaha player has six hands, and the flop will usually give him a lot of outs, he doesn't have to select his starting hand based solely on his position. He'll usually be getting the right odds to play weaker hands in earlier position than a hold 'em player would. Knowing that a player might have a preference for certain types of hands (psychology) doesn't help you all that much, because you still have to have the nuts or near nuts at the end of the hand. Knowledge of statistics or the mathematics of card distribution doesn't help you much, because most of the deck will be in play and there will be as many as forty combined hands against you.

Your main tool for reading hands in Omaha is simply knowing what hand is the current nuts, seeing which draws are possible, and realizing that it usually takes the nuts to win. It's that easy.

50. Tells are of less use. A **tell** is a clue from a poker opponent that helps you figure out what his hand is. The nature of Omaha means that all players who want to win the pot should be trying to make the nuts. A quick reading of the board will always tell you what hand that is. There will be no need for players to fake strength when they don't have it or to pretend to be weak when they have a strong hand. There won't be much acting going on. No matter how a player acts, he's still stuck with the true strength of his hand at the river, and he and everyone else knows it.

In my opinion, the best tell that the other players will give you in an Omaha game is simply their primary action — everyone knows what hand is the nuts and what the draws are, and yet they are still calling, betting, or raising. If you're trying to figure out a player's hand, all you need to know is that he's still playing.

To further round out your education on tells, here's a list of common hold 'em tells with explanations of how each one applies differently in an Omaha game:

1. Players with wheelchairs or walkers. These players are usually Tight/Passive hold 'em players because they don't like to take chances and go through their bankrolls. The physical act of going to get more chips might be

harder on them than having lost those chips to begin with. This tell does not apply too much in Omaha because you can predict that most (good) players will be tight players anyway.

2. Neatly dressed and conservative players. These people usually play a neat and conservative hold 'em game. Knowing this does not help much in Omaha because a player will have to play conservatively to beat you anyway. You'll know by the cards that he's holding at the end of a hand how he plays.

3. Impatient players. A player who is in a hurry to play the hand usually has a decent hand in hold 'em. This doesn't help in Omaha — the players should have decent hands anyway.

4. Mannerism changes. Players who have to stop what they're doing to play the hand usually have good starting hands. Seeing an Omaha player tell a spectator, "Don't bother me now because I have to play this hand," doesn't help you too much. He's supposed to have a good starting hand anyway.

5. Players showing their hands to spectators. In hold 'em this means it's usually a good hand. Again, seeing this doesn't help you too much, because he should be playing a good hand anyway. Besides, he's got six hands, and you can never know exactly how good any one of them is.

6. When a good player plays his first hand. This is a

good, reliable tell in both hold 'em and Omaha, but in Omaha, it doesn't tell you anything you didn't already know.

7. Players who stare at the flop. In hold 'em, this means that the player totally missed what he was hoping for on the flop. With six hands, that's harder to do in Omaha. If you see an Omaha player staring at the flop, it's more likely to be because he's trying to figure out all of the combinations he can make with his cards, not because he didn't flop anything.

8. Players who see the flop and then quickly look away. This is a good, reliable tell in both hold 'em and Omaha. It normally means that that player flopped a great hand or the nuts. In Omaha, that's what you'd expect anyway from someone, so you really haven't learned that much.

9. Players who cover their mouths. These players are usually bluffing in hold 'em. You know now that bluffing is not a big part of the game in Omaha, and you know why. If you see an Omaha player covering his mouth, it's more likely to be because he's yawning, not because he's bluffing.

10. Players who bet forcefully. In hold 'em, players who try to intimidate you by betting in an obviously over-confident style are often bluffing and trying to get you to check to them on the next round. This doesn't work in Omaha. Players will still have hands that they should bet for value on the next round anyway.

11. Directed bets. This is a variation of the last tell. A player who bets by throwing his chips at you instead of in the customary direction of the pot is trying to intimidate you, both in hold 'em and in Omaha. The purpose is to get you to fold on this or the next round. This works less well in Omaha. You will be forced to call more often than in hold 'em because of your greater number of outs and the (usually) much larger pot odds.

12. Players who stare at their opponents. In hold 'em, this happens at the river when a player has missed all of his draws and ends up with nothing. The stare is body language that means, "I missed my hand and I can't call a bet." This just doesn't happen in Omaha. A player who has nothing at the river knows very well that he can't bluff, he can't call a bet, and his opponent can't possibly have a worse poker hand than he does. Instead of staring so that he can have a chance to win a no-bet showdown, he'll usually check-fold and avoid the slight embarrassment of not having made his hand.

13. Players who immediately call your bet. This is usually a sign of a weak calling hand in hold 'em. You will see it less often in Omaha. Players with weak calling hands fold more often in Omaha. They know you're going to bet on the next round anyway.

14. Players who reach for their chips to call your bet before you can make the bet. This is done in hold 'em by a player who knows he will probably have to fold if you bet. He wants you to think that he can easily and quickly

call, and if you were planning to bluff you should save that bet. This tell does not occur much in Omaha. Players with weak hands will actually want to fold more often than in hold 'em. An Omaha player always knows what it takes to win; a hold 'em player can never be sure.

15. Undecided callers. Players who are genuinely undecided about calling your bet — and are not acting — usually have genuine borderline calling/folding hands in hold 'em. This will also hold true in Omaha; however, because of the fact that hand values have to be adjusted upward, the undecided Omaha player who does call your bet will have a much better hand than the hold 'em player in the same situation.

16. Deliberately flashed cards. A hold 'em player who "accidentally" flashes one of his cards usually does not have the hand that you would logically conclude he does. The most common use of this tell is when there are three hearts on the board and your opponent "accidentally" lets you see that he's holding the A♥. In hold 'em, this almost always means that his other card is not a heart. This tell does not occur in Omaha because there's no need to mislead anyone about the possibility of holding two suited cards. If you need to be holding the A♥ and any other heart to have the nuts, you don't need to convince your opponent that your one other card is also a heart. He already knows that any one of your other three cards is probably a heart.

17. Fabulous-looking flops. If the flop is A♠A♣K♦ and a hold 'em player not in the hand slaps his forehead

and rolls his eyes, you can be sure that he folded an ace before the flop. If the flop is Q♦T♦A♦ and he does the same thing, you can be sure he folded either the K♦ or J♦ before the flop. This doesn't happen as often in Omaha because big flops and big hands are much more commonplace, and everyone knows to wait for the river to decide what a big hand is anyway. Remember that all hand values have been adjusted upward.

18. Unnecessarily showing the nuts on the river. If you make the nuts in hold 'em and don't get called on the river, there's no need to show the hand. So why would you? You could just be proud of the hand, but you might also be doing so because you intend to bluff in the near future, and you want everyone to recall that you play only the nuts. This almost never happens in an Omaha game because, as you know by now, bluffing is a very small part of the game.

19. Visible disappointment. A player drawing to a big hand in hold 'em — especially when the pot is huge — will often show obvious, genuine disappointment if he does not make his hand by the river. He might fold out of turn or actually let you see his hand before the action is complete on the river. If you also missed your hand, this gives you an opportunity to pull off a bluff when you know you have almost 100% chance of success. This tell is of less value to you in Omaha. If your sole opponent has missed everything, you almost can't help but win the hand by default. You won't have to bluff. If this happens in hold 'em, you might win the hand. If it happens in Omaha, you

will win the hand.

20. Rabbit hunting. This is a reliable tell in both hold 'em and Omaha. Players who rabbit hunt (ask to see the next card after the hand is over) are usually bad players. The tell is not valuable to you — there are more reliable ways to tell who the bad players are. The best way is to just look at the cards they played when the hand is over.

Reading tells is a big part of the game at hold 'em. A hold 'em player can have any hand, and he will often have to beat only one other player on the river. He can trick you into believing one thing when another thing is true in an effort to get you to fold a better hand. This doesn't happen as much at Omaha. Omaha players can have six times as many hands, so an Omaha player knows in advance that he'll have to make the best possible hand to win the pot at the end.

51. It's more difficult to outplay your opponents. There are hundreds of combinations of strategies, tactics, tells, and moves that you can put on a player to make him fold or lose a hand when he had or might have made the best hand. These options are not available to you at Omaha. Your opponents will usually be getting the right odds to call to the river because of the pot size and the number outs they have. You're just going to need the best hand at the river to win the hand most of the time.

52. Misreading your hand is more common. Hold 'em players have only one hand of two cards that they can add to the board to make their hand. That's pretty easy to do. Omaha players have four cards with which to make six possible hands. Plus, they must use exactly two cards from their hand, and they can be playing for both high and low at the same time. That's complicated. It's easy to misread your hand. Even veteran players do so from time to time.

If you think you have any chance at all to win any part of the pot in Omaha, you should always turn all of your cards face-up at the showdown. Other players and the dealer will help figure out what you have, which will ensure that you don't lose any pots to which you were rightfully entitled. The dealer is required by poker room rules to read your hand before he mucks. You usually don't want to show everyone what you were playing at the end of a hold 'em hand, because you give away too much information to the enemy. That's not the case in Omaha.

53. "If it's possible, it's probable." This is a phrase frequently used to describe Omaha, and, as you can see by now, it's true. It's less true in hold 'em.

54. "You never know what you have 'til the river." Here's another popular saying about Omaha. With so many cards that make so many draws, you need to see how every hand turns out. That often takes all of the cards that you can get. When someone asks me if I know how to play Omaha, my stock answer is, "Yeah, isn't it that game where you have no idea what your hand is until you see the river card?" Rarely will an Omaha player make a hand on the flop or turn and say, "That's it. I don't need any more cards."

55. Ace-deuce is a good hand. A wheel is the best low hand, and the two best cards in the wheel to have in your hand are the ace and deuce. If there are three other low cards on the board and you don't get **counterfeited** (have your cards rendered useless when the board pairs them), you have the nuts. It's like making a royal flush for high. Ace-deuce is a big trap hand in hold 'em, because it makes it much harder to make a high hand that will win.

56. You can lose money with the nuts. It's called "getting quartered." This happens when you make the nut low hand and you have to split the low half of the pot with one or two other players. Imagine you have two low cards and you make the nuts on the river. You put $40 into the pot and so did two other players — to make a pot of $120.

At the showdown there is one winner for high and two winners for low (you being one of them). The pot is split — the high hand gets $60, and the two low hands split the $60 low pot. You get $30, but as I said, you just put $40 into the pot. You just made the nuts and lost $10. If you had to split it three ways, you'd get only $20, for a $20 loss. For this reason, it's usually best not to raise on the last round when it's three- or four-handed, unless you have the nut high hand and you know you don't have to split half a pot. This doesn't happen in hold 'em.

HOW OMAHA DIFFERS FROM HOLD 'EM

Summary

It's amazing how adding just two more cards to a hold 'em hand affects every aspect of the game in so many different ways. This is the attraction of Omaha. It appears to be a simple game to play, but the expert knows better. Every hand looks like it could be a winner, and that's what creates the action. If you're a good hold 'em player, you'll also be a good Omaha player, as long as you understand how Omaha differs from hold 'em, as I've shown you in this chapter.

I just explained to you how Omaha differs from hold 'em in *fifty-six* different ways. Don't forget that if you could arrange them into order of importance, skill at hand selection would certainly be #1. Good luck!

4

READING YOUR OMAHA HAND: HIGH

In any poker variation, knowing how to read your hand with confidence is a skill as important as understanding the strategy and theory of poker itself. It doesn't do any good to expertly apply the strategy and tactics of poker in the play of a hand if it turns out that you don't actually have the hand that you thought you had while you were playing it.

Misreading your hand is just as costly as deliberately playing badly, and how profitable is that? A cursory or summary look at the need to correctly read your hands won't do either. You need to look at this as an entirely separate skill — one that's just as important as understanding position, pot odds, semi-bluffing and raising.

Another way that Omaha differs from hold 'em is that being able to read your hand in Omaha, especially on the river, is a skill that takes a great deal of time and experience to develop. It doesn't always come as easy and quickly as it might have in hold 'em. Being able to read your hand in hold 'em is something you learned as a part of the game — while you were concentrating on mastering other parts of the game. Being able to read your hand at Omaha is a *major* skill. It's so important that it deserves its own chapter.

There are two purposes of the next three chapters:

1. To make you realize that this subject deserves your serious attention.
2. To provide you with examples of practice hands designed to help you avoid the common pitfalls of reading Omaha hands.

Omaha players who've had thousands of hands and years of experience routinely misread their hands. It can happen to anyone. You don't have to play Omaha for very long before you'll see someone misread his hand in your game. This mistake is understandable, given that you have four cards in your hand, and the best possible hand changes radically with each new card added to the board.

What follows is a series of sample hands designed to help you learn how to read your Omaha hand. We're looking at high hands first, and these are arranged in order, starting with a hand that makes one pair and working up the poker scale of hands from there. After that, we'll take a look at low hands, and then at hi-low split.

There are three main things that will help you read your Omaha hand, so keep these in mind:

1. Don't forget the two-card rule. Every hand you make

must contain *exactly* two cards from your hand.

2. The two-card rule, of course, means that you will always be using exactly three cards on the board.

3. All poker hands are made up of exactly five cards. Keep this in mind when trying to add that pair in your hand to the straight on the board.

To help you see each high example more clearly, I have drawn boxes around the two cards that you will be playing out of your hand and the three cards you will use on the board.

1.   Your hand is:

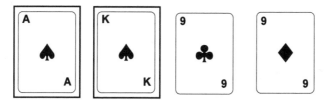

The board is:

Your hand is a pair of aces with a K Q J. You do not have two pair — aces and 9s — because that would mean using three cards out of your hand.

2.   **Your hand is:**

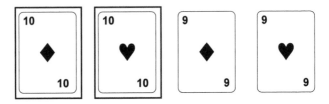

The board is:

Your hand is a pair of tens with an A K J. You don't have two pair — you can use only two cards in your hand.

3.   **Your hand is:**

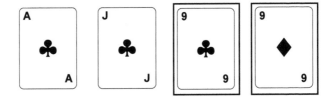

The board is:

READING YOUR OMAHA HAND: HIGH

Your hand is a pair of 9s with an 8 7 6. You do not have a 9-high straight, because there are no two cards in your hand that you can add to the cards on the board to make a straight. You do not have a flush, because you can use only two of the clubs in your hand, and there are only two more clubs on the board.

4.   Your hand is:

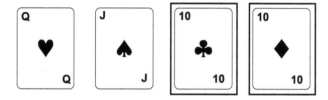

The board is:

You have two pair: tens and 7s with a 5 kicker.

5. **Your hand is:**

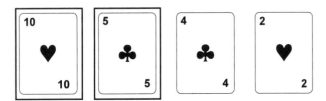

The board is:

You have two pair: 7s and 5s with a ten kicker. You can also make a pair of 4s and a pair of deuces, but you wouldn't, since the 7s and 5s are higher.

6. **Your hand is:**

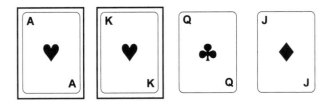

The board is:

Your hand is two pair: aces and kings with a queen kicker.

7.   **Your hand is:**

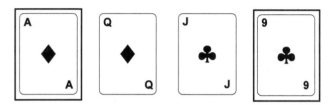

The board is:

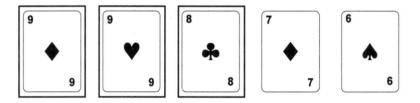

Your hand is three 9s with an ace and an 8. No straight is possible. In Omaha, as in all other forms of poker, you cannot make a straight without a ten or a 5.

8.   **Your hand is:**

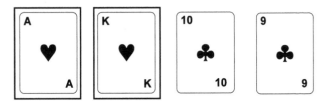

The board is:

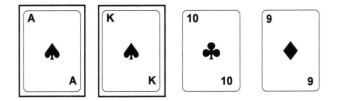

You have three jacks with an A K.

9.   **Your hand is:**

The board is:

READING YOUR OMAHA HAND: HIGH

You might think that you have a full house if you think you can add the ace in your hand to the one on the board to make jacks full of aces. You can't. You'd be using only one card from your hand. Your hand is just three jacks with an A K.

10. **Your hand is:**

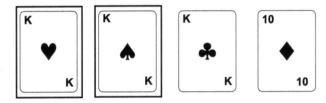

The board is:

I see four kings! Three kings in your hand and one on the board makes four kings. The problem is that you can play only two of the kings in your hand to go with the one on the board. Your hand is three kings with a J T.

11.   Your hand is:

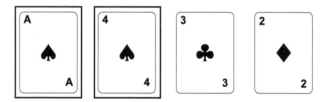

The board is:

There's a straight on the board, but you can't play it because you have to use two cards out of your hand. The two best cards you have are the A♠ and the 4♠ to make ace-high (A Q J T 4).

12.   Your hand is:

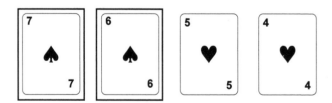

The board is:

You do have a straight, but it's not queen-high (as it might look at first glance). It's only ten-high due to the low cards in your hand.

13.   Your hand is:

The board is:

You have a straight, but it's only jack-high. The 8 in your hand replaces the 8 on the board. You cannot make a queen-high straight, because that would mean using six cards to make the hand.

14.   **Your hand is:**

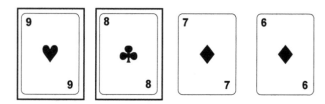

The board is:

You have a queen-high straight. The 9 8 in your hand replaces the 9 8 on the board.

15.   **Your hand is:**

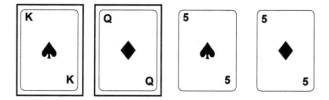

The board is:

You can beat the board by using your K Q to make a king-high straight.

16. **Your hand is:**

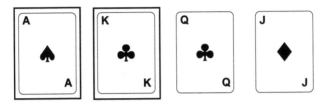

The board is:

The A K in your hand makes the nut straight. With this board, someone else could tie, but no one could beat you.

17. **Your hand is:**

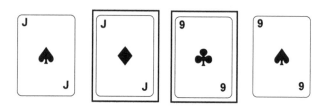

The board is:

You can make three jacks or three 9s, but you can't make a full house of jacks- or 9s-full because you'd have to use more than two cards from your hand. However, you can use one jack and one 9 from your hand to replace the jack and the 9 on the board —so you can make a Queen-high straight.

18. **The board is:**

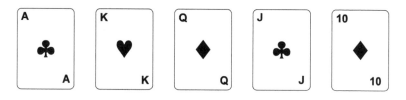

This is a common example that's easy to understand. Whenever there is an ace-high straight on the board, and no flush is possible, all you need to have the nuts is to hold two of the ranks of cards on the board in your hand. If you hold A K, A Q, A J, A T, K Q, K J, K T, Q J, Q T or J T in your hand, you can use these two cards to replace the two on the board and make the ace-high straight.

If the board is K♠Q♣J♥T♦9♣, you will have the king-high straight if you have any two of the cards on the board in your hand. The problem is that anyone holding an ace and one of the top four cards on the board (A K, A Q, A J, A T) will have the ace-high straight to beat you.

19. Your hand is:

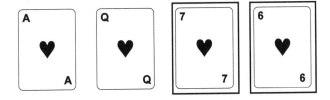

The board is:

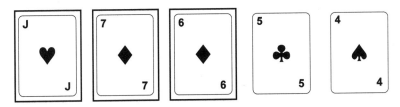

You have four hearts in your hand and one on the board, but you don't have a flush. Remember, you can use only two hearts from your hand. You have two pair: 7s and 6s with a jack kicker.

20. **Your hand is:**

The board is:

You have three hearts in your hand and two more on the board, but you can't make a flush because you must use only two cards from your hand and three on the board. There must be three or more of a suit on the board to make a flush possible. You can't make tens full of jacks, because you'd be using three cards from your hand. Your hand is three tens with a J6.

21. **Your hand is:**

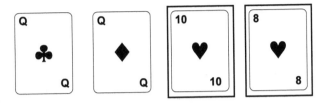

The board is:

Your hand is a flush consisting of A♥K♥T♥8♥6♥. You meet the requirements of playing two cards from your hand and three cards from the board, and you have a five-card hand. However, you do not have the nut flush, even though the A♥ is on the board. Anyone holding the Q♥ or the J♥ and another ♥ will have you beat.

22. **Your hand is:**

The board is:

Now you have the nut heart flush, because you hold the A♥ and another heart in your hand. Because each player gets to use nine cards to make his hand, you should be wary when three, four, or even five cards of the same suit appear on the board. Straight flushes are easier to make at Omaha. If you have a flush, you should also be on the lookout for the straight flush, either in your hand or someone else's hand.

23. **Your hand is:**

The board is:

You do not have a flush, because you don't have two hearts in your hand. Your A T gives you an ace-high straight.

24. **Your hand is:**

The board is:

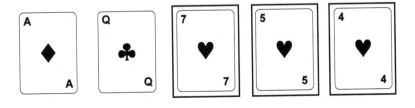

You have three aces and three queens, but you also have a flush. Anyone holding the 8♥6♥ or 6♥3♥ would have a straight flush. Any time you make the ace-high flush, as I've said, you should automatically check for straight flush possibilities.

25. Your hand is:

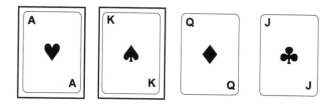

The board is:

Although you would have a full house in hold 'em, you don't in Omaha. If you could use only one card from your hand, you'd have kings full of 8s, but you can't do that. Your hand is three kings with an A 8.

26. **Your hand is:**

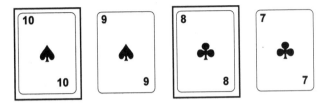

The board is:

Just as in the above example, you can't add the 8 in your hand to the board to make a full house. You have to add the 8 and another card. You have three 8s with a K T.

27. **Your hand is:**

The board is:

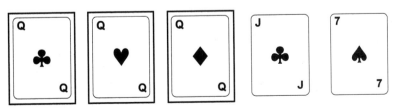

There's a three-of-a-kind on the board, and you have two cards in your hand that can each pair a card on the board to make a full house. But that's not possible. Adding the jack or the 7 to make the full house would be playing only one card from your hand. Your hand is three queens with an A K.

Tip: Whenever there is a three-of-a-kind on the board, you need a pocket pair to make a full house. There are no exceptions to this rule so you can commit it to memory. If no one held the Q♠ (to make four-of-a-kind) then the player who held the highest pair in his hand would have the highest full house.

28.   Your hand is:

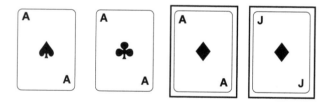

The board is:

You do not have a full house, because to make one, you'd have to use two aces and the J♦ from your hand, and that's three cards. The best two cards you can use are the J♦ and one of the other aces. Three-of-a-kind and a pair makes a full house at hold 'em, but that's not always the case in Omaha. Your hand is three jacks with an A 9.

29.   Your hand is:

The board is:

You have a full house: jacks full of 9s. You're playing two cards from your hand and three cards on the board. This holding also makes the nuts.

30.   **Your hand is:**

The board is:

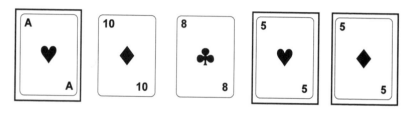

You have a full house: aces full of 5s. With the two aces in your hand, you have the nut full house. This is a great hand in hold 'em, but you must be aware that it's a little easier to beat in Omaha. A hold 'em player might have made only 5s full against you on the river (holding A 5, T 5, or 8 5) but an Omaha player who's holding a 5 might also have the other 5 to go with it to make four-of-a-kind.

31.   **Your hand is:**

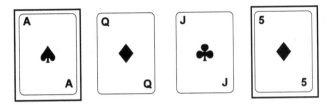

The board is:

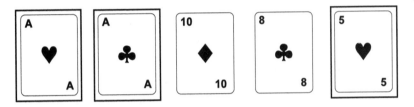

All of the cards I used in the previous example appear again in this example. The only difference is that I have exchanged the A♣ in your hand for the 5♦ on the board. You still have the same hand: aces full of 5s. The difference now is that you no longer have the nut full house. Anyone holding A T or A 8 will beat you, and anyone holding A 5 will tie you.

In Omaha, as in hold 'em, the true strength of your hand is relative and situational. A full house ranks high on the list of poker hands, but once you make the full house, you must then reevaluate it in light of the other cards on the board and of how many hands are against you.

32. **Your hand is:**

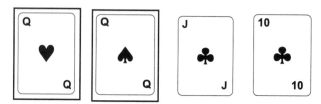

The board is:

This is a full house: 9s full of queens. If no one holds the 9♦ (to make four-of-a-kind), then whoever has the highest pocket pair has the highest full house. Anyone holding A A or K K would beat your hand in this example.

33. **Your hand is:**

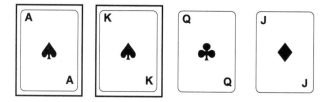

The board is:

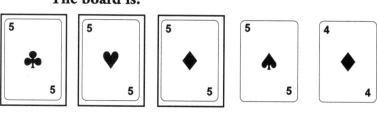

READING YOUR OMAHA HAND: HIGH

The odds against any four-of-a-kind being on the board are 4,164 to 1. If you play Omaha 40 hours a week, you will see four-of-a-kind on the board about once every three weeks. So, I'm now teaching you specifically how to play your hand in this one very rare circumstance. What I'm getting at is the bizarre rule regarding four-of-a-kind, and here it is: if there is a four-of-a-kind on the board, you cannot make four-of-a-kind as your poker hand! You'd have to play four cards on the board, and you can't do that. In this example, your hand is three 5s with an A K.

34.   Your hand is:

The board is:

Your hand is four 5s with a 4 kicker. Remember to be aware of straight-flush possibilities and the requirements to hit the jackpot. To be eligible for a jackpot, most poker rooms require that any four-of-a-kind (or better hand) be beaten by a higher hand. Some poker rooms set the minimum at four 7s, so it is wise to check before playing.

35. **Your hand is:**

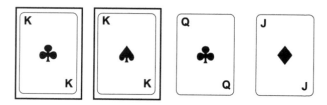

The board is:

Your hand is four kings with a jack kicker. A king plus the jack from your hand makes a full house — kings full of jacks — but that's not permitted because it doesn't make your best possible hand.

36. **Your hand is:**

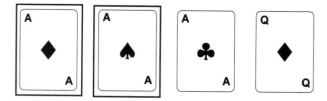

The board is:

Even though you're looking at all four aces, you have a relatively weak hand. Your hand is three aces with a K T. Anyone holding two hearts, Q J, J 7, or 7 6 will beat you.

37. **Your hand is:**

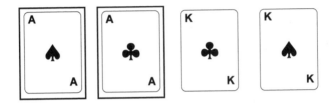

The board is:

There's a straight flush on the board, but all you have is a pair of aces. There are no two cards in your hand that you can play to make a straight flush, a flush, or even a straight.

38. **Your hand is:**

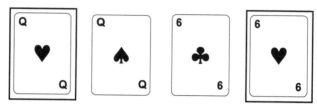

The board is:

You have both ends of the straight flush covered, but you do not have a straight flush. You have a queen-high flush: Q♥J♥T♥9♥6♥.

39. **Your hand is:**

The board is:

You don't have two hearts in your hand, so you can't make a flush. You have a ten-high straight.

40. Your hand is:

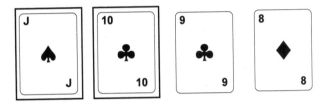

The board is:

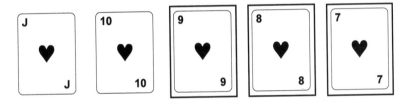

All four of your cards are paired, but if you said you had two pair, you'd be wrong. You can use any two cards in your hand to make a jack-high straight.

5

READING YOUR OMAHA HAND: LOW

Until the early part of the twentieth century, poker was always played for high. Then someone got the idea that there would be more action in the game if people played it for high and low at the same time. The lowest possible hand was determined to be 7 5 4 3 2 of at least two different suits. No ace was allowed in the hand, because an ace was considered to be a high card, and the hand starts with a 7 because that keeps it from being a straight. This game originated in Kansas City, so games played using this low hand were called Kansas City lowball.

In the 1960's, someone got the idea to change the lowest possible hand and create it out of the five lowest cards, A 2 3 4 5 (called a wheel or a bicycle). It was decided that, by rule, straights and flushes would have no significance when playing for low. A low hand would therefore always be your five lowest unpaired cards, and if those also happened to make a straight or flush, that would be irrelevant. For example, A♥2♥4♥6♥7♥ is an ace-high flush, but it is also a 7 6 4 2 A low hand. A hand made of A♦2♠3♣4♥5♦ is a 5-high straight, but is also a 5 4 3 2 A for low. Games using a wheel as the lowest possible hand were called California lowball because, well...you can figure that one out.

A decade later, people realized that they needed a qualifier for low, and it was decided that the hi-low game could use another adjustment. A new rule was added to the game: if you were playing for low, all five of your low cards had to be an 8 or lower. The addition of that rule means that the highest qualifying low hand is now 8 7 6 5 4, and the best low hand is still a wheel. If you start out with a hand like A♥3♦5♠6♣, you need one more card that is an 8 or lower and does not pair you (2, 4, 7, or 8) in order to have a low hand. Don't forget that in Omaha, three of those low cards must be on the board. This means that you always have to draw to make a low hand, and sometimes you won't make your draw.

The attraction of a hi-loww game lies in the fact that you can never be sure what it will take to win for high, but you always know what it takes to win for low. This takes away some of the skill needed to be a good poker player. When you're playing for high, you have to pay attention to your position, your opposition, the sequence of events before the flop, your hand selection, and your estimation of how the flop might have hurt you or helped everyone else. You have to do all of these things before you can determine if you have a good hand or not.

If you're playing for low, however, all you need to know is that the rules of the game will tell you if you have a good beginning hand or not. It takes a lot less skill to play for low, which adds significantly to the action. This isn't to say that playing for low is a bad thing or an element you'd rather not have in your game. Instead, it's a great feature of the game. It will add substantially to the hourly win rate of the player who understands how to take advantage of it.

Don't forget that you can still use only two cards from your hand. You must use exactly three cards from the board, and your hand must consist of exactly five cards. Poker games played today for low or hi-low use the California lowball scale, so a wheel is always the lowest hand you can make.

In the next fifteen practice hands, your Omaha hand is going to be an ace and a deuce with two other high, irrelevant cards. If it helps, you can think of these two extra cards as K♣Q♣ — cards that are obviously of no help for low. I'm using these cards to make the examples more simple and clear. Remember, you're trying to make only the low hand here.

For the purpose of teaching you how to read low hands, I'm first going to use only two low cards in your hand (A 2 X X), then three low cards (A 2 3 X), and then four low cards (A 2 3 4). *Since suits are irrelevant when playing for low, I will depict these hands with just letters and numbers, not actual playing cards.* If you already know how to play for low, or you already know how to play Omaha hi-low, then you will also have an opinion about what kinds of poker hands these examples are. I'm not going to say anything about hand selection, strategy, odds, or advisability of playing these hands in this section. I'm using these examples only as a tool for teaching you how to read the board for low. This is to keep it simple and to focus on the lesson at hand, which is to learn how to read low hands.

Specific advice, comments about odds, lessons on how and why to play certain hands, and strategy tips will be covered in detail in the next three chapters.

41.   Your hand is A 2 X X. The board is 9 Q K.
For a low hand to be possible eventually, the board must have at least one low card (8 or lower) on the flop. When all three cards on the flop are a 9, T, J, Q or K, no low will be possible for anyone. Even if two good, low cards came on the turn and river, you'd have only four low cards, and your fifth best low card would be a 9. You can't qualify for low this hand because your best possible low hand is a 9-low, and it takes an 8-low or better to qualify.

42.   Your hand is A 2 X X. The board is A T J.
When there's one low card on the flop, a low could be possible if the turn and river cards were also low cards that did not pair you. In this example, however, the ace on the board pairs the ace in your hand, and that means that you now have only one low card in your hand to work with. Even if the turn and river cards were a 3 and 4, the best low hand you could make would be A 2 3 4 T. That doesn't qualify for low — you need all five of the cards in your poker hand to be an 8 or lower.

43.   Your hand is A 2 X X. The board is 2 9 Q.
There's at least one low card on the flop but, just as in the above example, it has paired one of your low cards. It is not possible for you to make a low hand with this flop. There are no two cards that can come on the turn or river to give you an 8 or better for low.

44.   Your hand is A 2 X X. The board is A 2 Q.
There are two low cards on the flop, but they pair both of your low cards. This flop gives you something to work with for high, but you cannot make a low hand.

45.   Your hand is A 2 X X. The board is 7 T K.
There is one low card on the flop, and it did not pair you. A low is possible here, if the turn and river are two more low cards that don't pair your A 2 or one of the low cards on the board. If you do make a low here, it will be the nut low hand.

46.   Your hand is A 2 X X. The board is 9 Q K 3.
It is not possible to make a low with this board. Making a low was already impossible on the flop, when all three cards were above an 8. There is no card now that can come on the river to give you five cards to an 8 or lower.

47.   Your hand is A 2 X X. The board is A T J 4.
There are two low cards on the board and two in your hand; however, one of them is paired, and there's only one more card to come. You cannot make a low hand (as you should have realized on the flop).

48.   Your hand is A 2 X X. The board is 2 9 Q 6.
You're in the same situation here as in the above example.
The only difference is that your deuce is paired instead of
the ace. You cannot make a low with this hand.

49.   Your hand is A 2 X X. The board is A 2 Q 7.
You have two pair with only one other low card — the 7.
You cannot make a low with only one more card to come.
Even if the river were a 3 (the best card you could get),
your low would be A 2 3 7 Q. That doesn't qualify.

50.   Your hand is A 2 X X. The board is 7 T K 3.
A low is still possible at this point, and you will have the
nuts if the river card is a 4, 5, 6 or 8. If it is any other card,
you will be left with only four low cards and no qualifying
low hand.

51.   Your hand is A 2 X X. The board is 9 Q K T J.
No low is possible with this board. An A 2 can make the
nut low, but only if you get the right three cards on the
board. There are no low cards on this board.

52.   Your hand is A 2 X X. The board is A T J 4 9.
There are only two low cards on this board, and one of
them has paired your hand. All you can make here is
A 2 4 9 T.

53.   Your hand is A 2 X X. The board is 2 9 Q 6 5.
There are five low cards here; however, your deuce is
paired. With only four low cards, you can't make a low
hand.

54.   Your hand is A 2 X X. The board is A 2 Q 7 3.
Both of your low cards were counterfeited on the flop, leaving you with no low draw. Your lowest hand is a non-qualifying A 2 3 7 Q.

55.   Your hand is A 2 X X. The board is 7 T K 3 6.
You have the nut low hand. You needed to catch three low cards between a 3 and an 8 on the board, and you got them.

In the next fifteen examples, your hand will be A 2 3 X, with the X being a high, irrelevant card. The flop, turn, and river cards will be the same as in the previous examples. The only difference between the last examples and these ones is the addition of one more low card (the 3) to your hand. Notice how much more it adds to your possibilities whenever a low is possible.

Instead of individually listing all of the possible low cards, I will use "L" (Low) as shorthand to denote any low card that helps you. For example, if your hand is A 2 3 4 and the fifth card is a 5, 6, 7, or 8, I will call your hand A 2 3 4 L.

56.   Your hand is A 2 3 X. The board is 9 Q K.
You didn't get a low card on the flop. That rules out the possibility of any low for you or anyone else.

57.   Your hand is A 2 3 X. The board is A T J.
Your ace has been counterfeited, but you still have a possible low hand with the ace on the board and the 2 3 in

your hand.

58.   Your hand is A 2 3 X. The board is 2 9 Q.
This example is the same as #57, except that your deuce
has been counterfeited instead of your ace. If the right
cards come on the turn and river, you can still make a
low with the A 3 in your hand. Your hand would then be
A 2 3 L L.

59.   Your hand is A 2 3 X. The board is A 2 Q.
The board has paired two of your hole cards, but your
hand is better than it initially looks. You can still make
a low if you get any two other low cards on the turn and
river. If the last two cards are L and L, then your hand will
be A 2 3 L L.

60.   Your hand is A 2 3 X. The board is 7 T K.
A low is possible if you get two more low cards that do
not pair more than one of the low cards in your hand.
Your hand would then be A 2 L L 7, A L 3 L 7 or
L 2 3 L 7. Whenever you have three low cards in your
hand, you always have "one to give" if the board pairs one
of them.

61.   Your hand is A 2 3 X. The board is 9 Q K T.
No low is possible. To make a low, you must get at least
one low card on the flop.

62.   Your hand is A 2 3 X. The board is A T J 4.
You have a four-card low. You need one more low card on
the board that does not pair you. That would give you the

nut low: A 2 3 4 L.

63.   Your hand is A 2 3 X. The board is 2 9 Q 6.
Just as in the above example, you need one more low card that does not pair you. Your hand would then be A 2 3 L 6.

64.   Your hand is A 2 3 X. The board is A 2 Q 7.
If you get one more low card, you can make A 2 3 L 7 or A 2 3 L 7.

65.   Your hand is A 2 3 X. The board is 7 T K 3.
You need a low card that does not pair the A 2 in your hand or the 7 on the board. Your hand would then be A 2 3 L 7.

66.   Your hand is A 2 3 X. The board is 9 Q K T J.
No low is possible because there are not at least three low cards on the board.

67.   Your hand is A 2 3 X. The board is A T J 4 9.
You cannot make a low hand (although you had a chance before the 9 came on the river). There are only two low cards on the board — the ace and the 4 — and you need three.

68.   Your hand is A 2 3 X. The board is 2 9 Q 6 5.
You have the nut low hand: A 2 3 5 6.

69.   Your hand is A 2 3 X. The board is A 2 Q 7 3.
Because there are not three different low cards on the

board that you can use, you do not have a low. Being double-paired does not prevent you from making a low — as long as there are three other cards on the board that you can use.

70.   Your hand is A 2 3 X. The board is 7 T K 3 6.
You have the nut low, even though your 3 is paired. Your hand is A 2 3 6 7.

In the next fifteen examples, your hand will be A 2 3 4, and the boards will be the same as before. Notice how many more possibilities you have with four low cards than you had with just two.

71.   Your hand is A 2 3 4. The board is 9 Q K.
Even though you have four low cards in your hand, no low is possible. You still need to play three cards from the board.

72.   Your hand is A 2 3 4. The board is A T J.
Your ace is paired, but if you can get two more low cards without pairing more than one of the 2 3 4 in your hand, you will have the nut low. It will be A 2 3 L L, A 2 3 4 L, or A 2 3 4 L. All of these hands are the nuts.

73.   Your hand is A 2 3 4. The board is 2 9 Q.
Just as in the above example, you will make the nuts if you get two more low cards that don't pair you more than once. You will still have the nuts.

74.   Your hand is A 2 3 4. The board is A 2 Q.
You need one new low card that is not already in your hand or on the board. Your hand would then be A 2 3 4 L.

75.   Your hand is A 2 3 4. The board is 7 T K.
You can make the nut low with any two different low cards that come on the turn and the river, even if they pair the cards in your hand. Your hand would then be A 2 L L 7, A 2 3 L 7, A 2 3 4 7, A 2 3 L 7, A 2 3 4 7 or A 2 3 4 7.

76.   Your hand is A 2 3 4. The board is 9 Q K T.
No low is possible, as you should have realized when you saw the flop.

77.   Your hand is A 2 3 4. The board is A T J 4.
You can make a nut low hand if you get a low card that doesn't pair the ace or 4 on the board. That will give you three low cards with which to make a low. Your hand will then be A 2 3 4 L.

78.   Your hand is A 2 3 4. The board is 2 9 Q 6.
You can make a low if you get a low card that is not a 2 or a 6. An ace on the river would make your hand A 2 3 4 6, which is the nuts.

79.   Your hand is A 2 3 4. The board is A 2 Q 7.
You already have the nut low using the 3 and 4 in your hand. Your hand is A 2 3 4 7. You have the nuts. A 3 or a 4 on the river pairs you but does not kill your hand. It doesn't change your hand, but you no longer have the

nuts. With A 2 3 on the board, the nuts would be a 4 5, which you don't have. With an A 2 4 on the board, the nuts would be a 3 5, which you also don't have. You would still have a low, but it would no longer be the nuts.

80.   Your hand is A 2 3 4. The board is 7 T K 3.
You can make a low if you get another low card on the river. If an ace comes on the river, your hand is then A 2 3 4 7, which is the nuts. If the river card is a deuce, then your hand is A 2 3 4 7 — also the nuts.

81.   Your hand is A 2 3 4. The board is 9 Q K T J.
No low is possible because there aren't three low cards on the board.

82.   Your hand is A 2 3 4. The board is A T J 4 9.
You had the nut low draw with your 2 3. You needed a 5, 6, 7, or 8 on the river to have the nut low. At this point, your best hand is A 2 3 4 9. That doesn't qualify for low.

83.   Your hand is A 2 3 4. The board is 2 9 Q 6 5.
You have the nut low: A 2 3 5 6.

84.   Your hand is A 2 3 4. The board is A 2 Q 7 3.
You have a low hand with A 2 3 4 7, but it is not the nut low. Anyone holding a 4 5 would have the nuts with A 2 3 4 5.

85.   Your hand is A 2 3 4. The board is 7 T K 3 6.
You have the nut low with A 2 3 6 7.

READING YOUR OMAHA HAND: LOW

This concludes the practice reading low hands. As you can see, it can be tricky, confusing, and frustrating at times. If you'd like more practice, you should go over these hands again, and this time use the appropriate cards pulled from a deck of cards. It will help you to see your hand and the board using actual cards. You'll then physically be able to move the cards around to create a five-card hand, instead of just having to imagine it on paper.

6

READING YOUR OMAHA HAND: HI/LOW

This should be easy. All you have to do is figure out what the best high hand is and then determine what the best low hand is. Right?

Wrong! Even if you're new to hi-low, you should already realize that this is one of those things that's easy to describe in words but very difficult to put into practice. Easy to say; hard to do. It's like telling someone how easy it is to be a sculptor: all you have to do is start with a block of stone and chip away everything that doesn't look like your subject. Again, easy to say; hard to do.

Being able to read hi-low Omaha hands quickly and precisely is a skill that takes thousands of hands and countless hours at the table to develop. And even after that you're going to make a mistake once in a while. I play Omaha with a group of people who have more than two hundred years of collective experience at the game, and there's almost always at least one misread hand per playing session. As I said earlier, expertise at reading Omaha hands is a separate, major skill in itself.

There's a big difference between reading an Omaha hand for hi-low and reading it just for high or just for low. In hi-low, you must still use exactly two cards to make your high hand, and you must still use exactly two cards to make your low hand; however, they don't have to be the same two cards. There's still a two-card rule, but it's been modified. It's as if you're playing two different games at once (because you are) and you get to choose from your hole cards two different cards twice to make two different hands. This flexibility makes it easier to make both a high and a low hand, and it adds to the action and the enjoyment of playing the game.

Let's look again at the last five examples from above (#81-85) and see what hands you can make with them when you're playing for hi-low.

86.   Your hand is A 2 3 4. The board is 9 Q K T J.
You do not have a low hand because you can't meet the 8 qualifier. There's a straight on the board, but you can't play the board alone — you must use two cards from your hand. You don't have an ace-high straight because you don't also hold a ten, jack, queen or a king in your hand. Your high hand is A K Q J 4.

87.   Your hand is A 2 3 4. The board is A J T 4 9.
You don't qualify for low, and your high hand is A A 4 4 J. That's two pair — aces and 4s. The nut high hand would be an ace-high straight: T J Q K A.

88.   Your hand is A 2 3 4. The board is 2 9 Q 6 5.
Your low hand is A 2 3 5 6, which is the nut low. Your high hand is a 6-high straight: 2 3 4 5 6. You don't have the nut high hand; that would be 5 6 7 8 9.

89.   Your hand is A 2 3 4. The board is A 2 Q 7 3.
Your low hand is A 2 3 4 7. The nut low would be A 2 3 4 5. Your high hand is A A 3 3 Q. That's two pair — aces and 3s. The nut high is the same as the nut low: A 2 3 4 5.

90.   Your hand is A 2 3 4. The board is 7 T K 3 6.
You have the nut low: A 2 3 6 7. Your high hand is a pair of 3s (3 3 A K T). The nut high is 3 4 5 6 7.

None of the five examples you just looked at involved a possible flush, because I deliberately left out specific suits in order to keep the examples as easy as possible. The rest of the practice hands will include possible flushes.

91.   Your hand is:

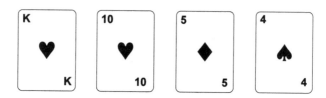

The board is:

Your low hand is A 2 3 4 5. Your high hand is a straight: T♥J♣Q♦K♥A♠. You have the nuts in both directions.

92.   Your hand is:

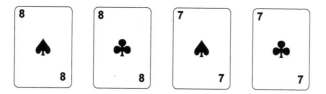

The board is:

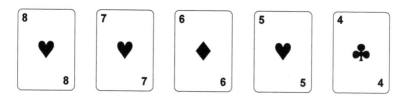

You flopped three 8s and three 7s, but your final high hand is 8♠7♠6♦5♥4♣ to make an 8-high straight. That's also your low hand, though it's the worst low you can make and still qualify for low.

93.   Your hand is:

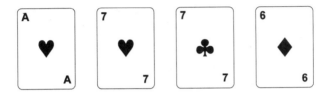

The board is:

You flopped three 7s and the nut flush draw. Your high hand is A♥K♥J♥7♥4♥, and that is the nut high. Your low hand is A 4 5 6 7.

94. **Your hand is:**

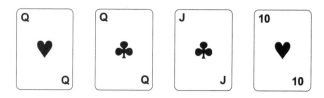

The board is:

You flopped three queens, but you do not have a full house even though you also paired your J♣ and T♥. To make a full house, you'd have to play three cards in your hand, and you can't do that. Your high hand is a queen-high straight: Q♥J♣T♦9♠8♠. Obviously, there's no low hand here.

95. **Your hand is:**

The board is:

You flopped three kings and a flush draw. Your high hand is a flush consisting of A♥K♥8♥6♥2♥. Your low hand is A 2 5 6 8.

96. **Your hand is:**

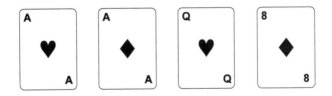

The board is:

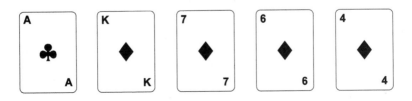

You flopped three aces and the nut diamond flush draw. Your high hand is A♦8♦7♦6♦4♦. Your low is A 4 6 7 8.

97.   Your hand is:

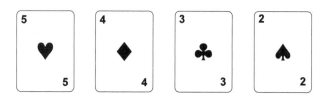

The board is:

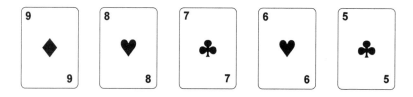

Your high hand is an 8♥7♣6♥5♥4♦, to make an 8-high straight. You cannot make a 9-high straight because there are no two cards in your hand that will stretch that far. Your low hand is 2 3 5 6 7.

98.   Your hand is:

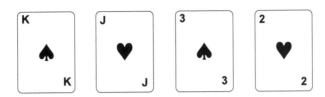

The board is:

Your high hand is A♠K♠Q♥J♥T♠, which is the nuts. Your low hand is A 2 3 4 5, which is also the nuts for low.

99.   Your hand is:

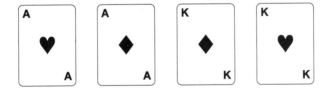

The board is:

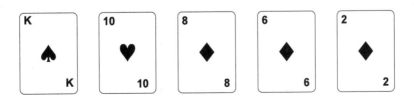

You have three kings, but you also have the nut flush, which is A♦K♦8♦6♦2♦. You cannot make a low hand because you don't have two low cards in your hand.

100.   Your hand is:

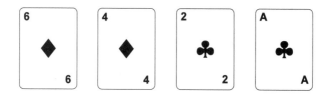

The board is:

Your high hand is the A♣K♣8♣3♣2♣ flush, which is the nuts because you hold the A♣ in your hand, and no straight-flush is possible. Your low hand is A 2 3 7 8, which is also the nuts. This is a nut-nut hand.

Summary

You might think that one hundred examples of how to read hands is a lot, but it's just a sign of how complicated Omaha hi-low split can be. That's what it took me to show you how you can make (and sometimes not make) every high hand and then all the possible lows. If you'd like more practice reading hands, I recommend you practice on your own with a deck of cards.

READING YOUR OMAHA HAND: HI/LOW

Give yourself four random cards, and use the next five cards off the top of the deck as the board. Determine what your best high and low hands are; then muck the five cards on the board. Use the next five cards off the top of deck for your new board. Repeat the exercise until you go through the deck. Then give yourself four new cards and repeat the process all over again. You might think that this procedure is a bit laborious; however, I can assure you that there is no less expensive or less time-consuming way to practice reading Omaha hands. Good luck!

OMAHA ODDS

Just like playing Omaha is more fun than playing hold 'em, knowing some Omaha odds is also a little more fun. After the flop you'll usually be trying to make more than just one hand, and you will usually have a large number of outs to make your hand. Consider this example:

Your hand is:

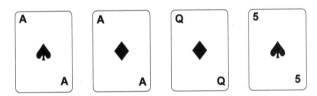

The board is:

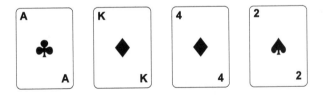

There's a lot going on here. You have a set of aces, and pairing the board would give you either the nut four-of-a-kind or the nut full house. You also have the nut four-flush diamond draw. Finally, you have the nut low draw, which would give you a low and a straight for high. Let's count your outs.

Let's say your hand is A♦A♠A♣X X. The A ♥ will give you four-of-a-kind. The 2♣, 2♥, 2♦, 4♣, 4♠, 4♥, K♣, K♠, or K♥ will give you the nut full house. That's ten outs.

Your hand can also be A♦Q♦K♦4♦. In that case, the 3♦ will give you the nut flush (and, used with the 2 and the 5 instead of the king and the queen, the nut low wheel hand). The 6♦, 7♦, and 8♦ will give you the flush and a low. The 5♦, 9♦, T♦, and J♦ will give you the nut flush. That's eight outs.

And what if your hand is A♦2♠4♦5♠? The 3♣, 3♠, and 3♥ will give you the nut low wheel, and the 6♣, 6♠, 6♥, 7♣, 7♠, 7♥, 8♣, 8♠, and 8♥ will all give you a low. That's twelve outs.

Any one of thirty of the forty-four unseen cards will improve your hand to four-of-a-kind, a full house, a flush, a straight or the nut low wheel with one card to come. And that's notwithstanding the fact that you already have a set of aces, which might win without improving. What makes Omaha fun to play is that these thirty outs are the outs that you will have against your opponents; in hold 'em it's your opponents who always have the thirty outs against you.

OMAHA DRAWING ODDS
FROM A DECK OF 45 UNSEEN CARDS

Number of Outs	2 Cards to Come	1 Card to Come
30	89.4%	68.2%
29	87.9%	66.0%
28	86.3%	63.6%
27	84.6%	61.4%
26	82.7%	59.1%
25	80.8%	56.8%
24	78.8%	54.5%
23	76.7%	52.3%
22	74.4%	50.0%
21	72.1%	47.7%
20	69.7%	45.5%
19	67.2%	43.2%
18	64.5%	40.1%
17	61.8%	38.6%
16	41.0%	36.7%
15	56.1%	34.1%
14	53.0%	31.8%
13	49.9%	29.6%
12	46.7%	27.3%
11	43.3%	25.0%
10	39.9%	22.7%
9	36.7%	20.5%
8	32.7%	18.2%
7	29.0%	15.6%
6	25.2%	13.6%
5	21.2%	11.4%
4	17.2%	9.1%
3	13.0%	6.8%
2	8.8%	4.5%
1	4.4%	2.3%

If you're already familiar with hold 'em odds, then you can see that the above table is similar to the one you'd use for hold 'em. The only difference is that there are forty-five unseen cards after the flop in Omaha, while there are forty-seven unseen cards after the flop in hold 'em. Because that's only a two card change, the percentages are not radically different. What is radically different about this table, however, is that you can have so many more outs after the flop in Omaha than you can in hold 'em.

There are a few things about this table that are worth mentioning. The first is the fact that you need only fourteen (or more) outs on the flop to have more than a 50% chance of making your draw. That's good news, because most of the hands you'll be playing will be multi-way draws. A high and a low draw, a straight and a flush draw, a low and a straight or flush draw, or a set and any other draw will always give you more than fourteen outs.

In hold 'em, the highest number of outs you can have on the flop is fifteen, and that would be on an open-end straight flush draw. The most common draws in hold 'em are a straight (8 outs), a flush (9 outs), and a set (10 outs). You should get accustomed to playing with the higher number of outs in Omaha. Hands that are good in hold 'em, like straight and flush draws, are definite dogs in Omaha if they're all you have working for you.

What I love about poker (and especially about Omaha) is that you're not playing against the house; you're playing against the other players at the table. As long as the game is **raked** (a percentage of each pot is taken by the casino), casino management doesn't care what your edge is over the other players.

The next chart shows the odds of making a low hand after the flop. It's a new kind of chart for you hold 'em players, because hold 'em is not played for hi-low, but Omaha is.

OMAHA 8 OR BETTER ODDS
ODDS OF MAKING A LOW AFTER THE FLOP

You Hold	Odds of Making 8 or Better Low
4 Different Low Cards	
Before the flop	49%
2 new low cards on flop	70%
1 new low card on flop	24%
3 Different Low Cards	
Before the flop	40%
2 new low cards on flop	72%
1 new low card on flop	26%
2 Different Low Cards	
Before the flop	24%
2 new low cards on flop	59%
1 new low card on flop	16%

Your best draws are when you have three or four low cards in your hand and you get two new low cards on the flop. Your worst draw is when you have two low cards in your hand and you get only one new low card in the flop.

A Few More Omaha Odds

There are 270,725 different four-card hands that you can be dealt in Omaha. If you ignore specific suits, that's just 5,277 hands.

50% of the players in the game will be holding a pocket pair before the flop.

The odds of being dealt any four-of-a-kind as your hand are 20,824-1.

You have a 70% chance of being suited in your first four cards. The odds that you will be double-suited are about 14%.

If you have a nut flush on the turn, the board will pair on the river 25% of the time. If you also have two of the cards on the board in your hand, the board will pair only 20% of the time.

The odds of one of any three of the thirteen ranks of cards coming on the flop are 46.3%. For example, if you hold A♠2♣3♥K♠ and you're hoping not to pair your A, 2, or 3, you will get an ace, deuce or trey on the flop 46.3% of the time.

If you hold two suited cards, you will end up with the flush 4.02% of the time. If you hold three suited cards, your odds go down to 3.58% (an 11% decrease), and if all four of your cards are suited, your odds go down further to 3.17% (a 21% decrease from the original).

OMAHA ODDS

The odds that you will hold a pocket pair are nine times greater in Omaha than in hold 'em. After you get your first card in hold 'em, there's only one more card to come to give you a chance to pair. After you get your third card in Omaha, there are still nine different cards that can pair one of your three pocket cards.

8

HAND SELECTION

Are you familiar with the Rorschach test? It's the one in which the psychiatrist shows you some inkblots and you're supposed to say what those inkblots suggest to you. I'd like to give you a verbal version of that test. I'm sure you're already familiar with the idea. If I say, "Economics," you might say, "Supply and demand." If I say, "Algebra," you might say, "A plus B equals C." Up-Down. Negative-Positive. Nouns-Verbs. Yes-No. If I say, "Omaha," I want you to say, "Hand selection." The two are that closely related.

Hand selection is what it's all about in Omaha. If you can't select your hands correctly, then ultimately nothing else matters. You'll have a great time, you'll make some big hands, and you might even win some big pots. In short, you'll have a great ride, but it will be a ride only as far away as the rail.

It's very popularly believed that the worst game you can play in a casino is the one that offers the worst odds to the player. What could be any worse than that? I'm here to tell you that the one thing that you can do that's worse than that is to play a game of skill without the skill. In that situation, you can literally give your money away faster than a casino can legally take it from you in any other game.

I'm not saying you shouldn't play Omaha. As I've said, it's a wonderful game with a far better edge than other games you'll find in the casino. But to play Omaha, you must have skill, particularly at hand selection. I'm now going to give you forty pointers to help you build your skill at Omaha.

40 Hand Selection Guidelines & Tips

1. Let's go back to that verbal version of a Rorschach test. If I then say to you, "Hand selection," I want you immediately to say, "Scoop the pot!" Your main objective when selecting which Omaha hand to play is to win all of the pot, not just half of it. If you play all high cards, then you don't want to see a possible low on the board, because you may win only high (and sometimes not even that). If you play low cards, you'd also like to make a straight or a flush so you can win both halves of the pot. Always think about how you can win more than just half of the pot.

2. You always want to draw to the nuts. Why deliberately try to make a second-best hand from the very beginning? It's very expensive to keep coming in second place in Omaha. You will sometimes backdoor odd hands, and you will sometimes win without having the nuts, but that should never have been your intention from the beginning.

3. It's true that position is less important in Omaha. That does not mean that you should routinely play obviously inferior hands for your position. The price may not be as high as it is in hold 'em, but there's still a price. You can still be punished for playing out of position. You should rely on your skill and understanding of the game to play intelligently — don't deliberately give away any advantages. Don't play less than your best game on purpose just because the cost appears to be minor.

4. You should know that, in a nine- or ten-handed limit game, only about 15% of all Omaha hi-low split hands are profitable in the long run. If you think about it, that should hold true for all other forms of poker as well. Once you start playing more than the top 15% of starting hands in draw, stud or hold 'em, you start getting into bigger swings in your hourly rate. You eventually will start having a negative hourly win rate. I'll show you in this chapter what those 15% winning hands are.

5. All four of your cards must work together. With four cards, you can make six different hands. Ideally, you'd like to be suited or double suited to maximize your flush possibilities, you want to have in your hand the ace of your suit, and if you don't hold a high pair, you want all four of your cards to be consecutive or close together to maximize your straight possibilities.

6. Every time you evaluate a hand you should ask yourself, "Does every card in this hand have a purpose?" Look at all six of the hands you can make with your four cards. Consider this hand: A♣2♥9♠K♣. The A 2 makes you a low and a possible wheel. The A K makes you the nut straight and nut flush, and the 9♠ makes you...a loser. Your hands are:

1. A♣K♣ - great hand
2. A♣2♥ - nut low draw, good hand
3. A♣9♠ - bad hand
4. K♣9♠ - 3-gapper, horrible hand
5. K♣2♥ - horrible hand
6. 9♠2♥ - horrible hand

Only two of your six combinations are any good. This hand is much, much worse than it looks, especially if you initially looked at it through the eyes of a hold 'em player.

7. Avoid **danglers**. A dangler is a card that doesn't fit in with the other three cards in your hand. It cuts the number of your playable combinations down from six to three. That's too much to give away to your opponents.

8. If you do have to play a hand with a dangler (you might be in the blind or on the button with incredible pot odds), make sure that you have multiple draws and that they are to the nuts. If you're going to handicap yourself *deliberately*, you might as well make sure you get compensated for it. Pocket aces with a suited deuce would be the nut low and nut flush draw. That's probably a playable hand in late position.

9. A card that's a dangler but does add a little something to your hand is what I call a **half-dangler**. A♥K♦K♠7♠ is a good example. The 7♠ is a dangler, but it does add a possible king-high flush draw to your hand. It is all right to play hands with half-danglers if all of the other game conditions are favorable to you. If you're in late position, you don't have to call any pre-flop raises, everyone has called, and there's little prospect of a raise behind you, that would be a perfect time to play a hand with a half-dangler.

The reason you'd even consider playing a half-dangler is that you must face the reality of the game. Ideally, you want your starting hand to be perfect in every way. There are easily two dozen different criteria that a starting hand must meet to be perfect. Some of them are contradictory. If you waited for only the theoretically perfect hands to come along, you might play only one hand per playing session, and when you did play, you'd get no action! Plus, the blinds would eat up your buy-in. You'd be playing way too tight, and you'd fall victim to the ploys that can be put upon too-tight players.

Obviously, this won't do. You're going to have to strike a balance and get in there and play a hand once in a while. The next best hand after the perfect hand is the hand with the half-dangler. If you choose wisely, you can still show a profit by playing these hands.

10. Be aware of stopping yourself. If you have a hand like J♠J♣J♥T♣, you should probably not play the hand. Your odds of flopping a set are exactly half of what they would be without the extra jack in your hand. Not one of the thirteen different possible four-of-a-kinds is playable.

A♥2♥2♦2♣ might be an okay hand to play, since you have the nut low with three of the deuces locked up, and you have the nut flush draw. A♦A♥A♣ with a suited ten, jack, queen or king might be all right if other game conditions were favorable.

There's also the well-known phenomenon of having three or four cards of the same suit in your hand. This obviously cuts into your odds of making the flush, as I explained in the previous chapter; however, this hand is not as bad as it's been made out to be. If you are sure that the hand has other quality draws (as A♥2♥4♥Q♥ does, for example) then I think you can see the flop with it. If your hand is 5♣7♣8♣T♣, then you have a lousy hand and should not play.

11. All hands you play should give you more than one draw. Making one type of hand while drawing to an even better hand is the essence of being a winner at Omaha. The worst thing you can do is flop a straight with no other draws or no other way to improve the hand after that. If you hold 6♠8♣9♥J♦ and flop a straight, you have a very vulnerable hand. Every card that can come on the turn and river can beat you. Good players have learned to show a profit in this situation by folding! So should you. There are two acceptable exceptions to this guideline: if you're holding the four lowest cards (A 2 3 4) or the four highest cards (A K Q J). In those cases, you can't be beat for low, and your straight can't be beat by another straight for high.

12. You need to recognize the value of being suited or double suited. That's very important because being suited or double suited adds to your win rate and hourly rate more than any other factor. For every hand you win when you're not suited, you'll win four times as many when you're suited and five times as many when you're double suited. Most Omaha players underrate the value of being suited. (It's also, of course, a major plus if you hold the ace of your suit.)

13. When playing for high, you should keep in mind that there are really only three different poker hands for you to make: a straight, a flush, and a full house. These are all completed hands. Four-of-a-kinds and straight flushes are also completed hands, but you should look at them as bonus hands. They're not your initial, primary objective. If you make four-of-a-kind or a straight flush, it should usually be because you were first trying to make a flush or a full house.

When selecting hands to play, I recommend that you play hands that can make the top two of these three hands — the flush and the full house. (If your flush draw also gives you a straight draw, so much the better.) Hands with a suited ace and a pocket pair could make a flush or a full house. A pocket pair with other straight cards or two suited cards with straight cards could make the other two combinations of hands. The other two combinations — straight and full house and straight and flush — are less desirable because those are obviously weaker hands.

14. Two good hold 'em hands do not always make a good Omaha hand. You have to look and see what four other Omaha hands those two hold 'em hands make. If your hand is K♦K♥8♠7♠, you have two easily recognizable hold 'em hands. K♦K♥ and 8♠7♠ are both good hold 'em hands. The four other Omaha hands they make are K♦8♠, K♦7♠, K♥8♠, and K♥7♠. A hand that looks pretty good at first glance looks pretty ridiculous now, doesn't it?

15. If the above is true, then an Omaha hand that contains only one good hold 'em hand is unquestionably unplayable. A lot of hold 'em players, myself included, have a favorite hold 'em hand. When we see those cards in our Omaha hands, we are tempted to play. Why play only one card combination when everyone else is playing six combinations?

16. Don't fall in love with A A X X. Don't automatically play this hand every time you get it just because it's a pair of aces. This is an extension of the above advice, but even if you don't have a favorite hold 'em hand, don't fall for this one because you think, "A pair of aces has got to be good in any game, even Omaha." Ordinarily, you'd be right, but since Omaha is not an ordinary game, you'd be wrong in this case. Which values those X X cards are is very important. These cards will tell you whether or not you can play the hand.

17. When you're playing hi-low split, avoid playing pocket pairs of 8s and below if you're playing them to make the set. If you flop a set of 2s through 8s, it will make a low hand possible. That low card will encourage all of the low draws to chase their hands, which could turn into straights and flushes to beat you. You're in the exact same situation when you flop a set of aces, but that's a problem you'll just have to live with.

18. Conversely, it is good to play pocket pairs of 9s and higher. If you make your set, no low draw may be possible. You also have the added equity of usually having the higher set when another player plays his lower pocket pair. Playing only the higher pocket pairs will keep you out of the losing end of set-over-set confrontations, which are always very costly.

19. Be aware of the requirements to hit the jackpot. I play Omaha at one of the best card rooms in the country, and the jackpot requirements there change by the month. The last time I was there, a player had to lose with four 7s or better to win the jackpot. I usually play only pocket 9s and higher; however, that day I also played pocket 8s and 7s. With a possible $8,000 added to every pot, it was mathematically correct to accept the small extra risk of losing the hand to win the jackpot.

20. If your starting hand is two small pair, you should usually not play unless it is A A 2 2, A A 3 3 or 2 2 3 3. With all other small pairs, you usually can't win for high and you can't win for low. A small pair makes a small set, which in turn makes a small full house. A hand like that might win at hold 'em, but not at Omaha.

21. If you play a pocket pair, it helps if the other two cards are close in rank (to give you a straight draw if you make the set). This might seem like obvious advice, but it sometimes helps to be reminded of the obvious in advance. For example, a holding of 7♣8♥8♦9♠ gives you more outs and options than a hand like 3♣8♥8♦K♠.

22. In high games, play only the highest cards. Make sure that your straight and flush draws are to the nuts. In hi-low split games, play the highest and the lowest cards. Stay out of the middle. Remember, you're playing hi-low, not high/middle/low. If you insist on playing the cards in the middle, your stack of poker chips will eventually be divided up between the players who do play only the highest and lowest cards.

23. The worst cards you can have in your hand are the 7, 8, and 9. There are no combinations of starting hands that contain a 7, 8, or 9 that are winning hands in the long run. None! A A 9 9, A A 8 8, and A A 7 7 come close to being winning hands, and if you can play them in late position, you can probably show a small profit (due more to your position than to your cards). If you never played another hand with a 7, 8, or 9 in it for the rest of your life, you'd be reducing the big swings in your bankroll, and your hourly win rate would go up.

24. If the lowest card in your hand is a 4, 5, 6, 7, 8, or 9, then you have a losing hand. These cards are in the middle range. You will lose to players holding the aces, 2s and 3s for low, and you will lose to players holding the tens, jacks, queens, kings and aces for high. If the lowest card in your hand is between a 4 and a 9, you should not play the hand unless you have several good, specific, and compelling reasons to do so.

25. Your flush draws are more valuable to you if you have the ace of your suit in your hand but not the king and queen of your suit. When you make your nut flush, you will often be paid off by someone who made the king- or queen-high flush and was hoping that you didn't have the ace. If you hold A♦K♦Q♥6♦ and the board is Q♦8♦7♣5♠2♦, a player holding J♦9♦ is not going to call with his losing hand, even though he has a flush. If he's holding K♦9♦, however, he'll usually call all the way to the river, because it's possible that you don't have the A♦. Throwing away a completed flush on the flop is no big deal in Omaha.

26. You should not deliberately try to make a third-highest flush as the main objective of your hand. If there's no ace or king on the board, that would be a queen-high flush. A third-highest flush is usually okay only if it was a backdoor flush made while trying to make a different hand.

27. Aces are the key cards in Omaha hi-low split. You'll have one or more aces in your hand about 25% of the time. Of those hands, only about 55% will show a profit in the long run. Some players automatically play any time they hold an ace. As you just learned, this is an incorrect strategy. If you play a hand with an ace, it should also be because of the value of the other three cards.

28. There are very few winning Omaha hands that do not contain an ace. There are only nine of them — here they are:

1. K K Q Q
2. K K J J
3. K K T T
4. K K 2 3
5. K K 2 4
6. K K 3 4
7. 2 2 3 4
8. 2 2 3 5
9. 2 2 3 6

If you're surprised to learn that there are only nine ace-less winning Omaha hands, then you're really going to be surprised at this: all of these hands have to be suited at least once to be profitable. Do you recall that I said earlier that a suited hand wins four times as often as the same unsuited hand? These hands are losers when they're not suited. It takes the extra value of winning with flushes to give these hands a positive expectation. There are only nine of these hands. If you're going to be an Omaha player for the rest of your life, I don't think it's too much for you to make the effort to memorize them.

29. Ace-deuce as your only two low cards is a horrible hand. If that's the only reason you have to play the hand, you should not play it. Because you always know what it takes to win for low (A 2 if you don't get counterfeited) a lot of players play every time they get that A 2, regardless of what their other cards are. That's a losing proposition, because several statistically improbable events have to take place in the correct order for you to end up with a low. And then you have to worry about splitting your share of the pot!

You have to get at least one new low card on the flop and end up with at least three low cards on the river. Then you can get an ace or deuce on the board. Finally, you have to be the only player in the game with an A 2. If you never again tried to play with A 2 as your only low cards, you would show a dramatic improvement in your hourly rate. Let the other players make the longshot draw; all you have to do is be there when they miss.

30. There is no one best high hand before the flop. The best hand is determined by a lot of variables, which include table tightness/looseness, the personalities of specific players, the time of day, the level of aggressiveness or passivity of your opponents, and your position. You could say that the best possible high hand changes with each new hand.

There is a highest pre-flop hand, however, and that is A A K K double suited. Don't hold your breath waiting to get this hand, because the odds against it are 45,120-1. This is the highest hand, but it's not the best hand. You have only two pair here, and your one straight draw will always be a **gutshot** (an inside straight draw). Gutshots are bad in hold 'em and even worse in Omaha. A better hand might be A A J T double suited. This hand makes it much easier to make a straight because you can make five different straights instead of just one.

31. The best pre-flop hi-low split hand is A A 2 3 double suited. With this hand, you will win some part of the pot about 42% of the time. Look at what you can make with A♠A♥2♠3♥:

> 1. Four Aces
> 2. A straight-flush in spades
> 3. A straight-flush in hearts
> 4. Aces-full
> 5. Several other small full houses
> 6. A♠-high flush
> 7. A♥-high flush
> 8. Suited wheel for a scoop hand
> 9. 6-high straight
> 10. The nut low

Talk about a hand where all the cards work together!

32. A 2 5 6 and A 2 6 7 are decent hands because they give you a chance to make the nut low wheel with a 6- or 7-high straight. That's important because although you'll have to split the low pot with anyone else who made the wheel, you'll be able to steal the entire high pot by having the 6 or the 6 7 in your hand. This is a common **nut-nut** hand (it gives you the nuts for both high and low.

33. A 2 7 8 and A 2 8 X are not good low hands. Ace-deuce by itself is not a good hand. A lot of players recognize that fact, and they try to help the hand by playing another

HAND SELECTION

low card, even if it's the 7 or the 8. Yes, it does help (in theory) to have a third low card for backup; however, the 7 and the 8 are both so high that they are almost always of no real, practical help in an actual game. There will be times when the 7 or 8 does help you make a low and win the low side. These instances are so infrequent, however, that you cannot make up for all of the times you play it and lose. If you are a good Omaha player, these will be the cards that the other players will be holding when you win the low pot.

34. A 2 K Q is popularly believed to be a good hand because it contains the two highest and lowest cards in the deck — the A 2 and the A K. The logic is that you can make the nut low and the nut straight with this hand.

Here are the problems with this line of reasoning:

1. A low will be possible only one-half of the time.
2. After that, your ace or deuce will be counterfeited over 50% of the time.
3. If you do win low, you will be quartered about 33% of the time, which means you will have made the nuts but lost money on the hand.
4. You will make the nut high straight and not be beat by a flush or full house only about 3% of the time.
5. You will then be quartered for high about 33% of the time.

This is a hand that requires you just to hope that the cards on the board will be perfect, and that's not the way to play poker.

Tip: Any time you look at your Omaha hand (or any other poker hand, for that matter) and you think to yourself, "I can win with this, but first I need this to happen, then that, then the other thing..." and so on — *throw the hand away*. You can play better than that.

35. 2 3 4 5, 2 3 4 6, 2 3 4 7, and 2 3 4 8 are bad hands. They are much worse than they look. The 2 3 4 5 looks like it should be the near-perfect low hand. The problem is that you need one, specific card to come — the ace — and then after that you need two more low cards on the board. If three low cards come with no ace, then an A 2 can beat you, and that's very likely to happen. If your hand gets counterfeited, then A 3, A 4, and A 5 will beat you, and that also is very likely. If you do make the wheel, you'll usually get quartered. It's very hard to win the entire low pot with this hand. If you usually play these hands, you should try *not* playing them. You will see that most of the time you'll have made the best decision.

36. 3 4 5 6, 4 5 6 7, and 5 6 7 8 are horrible hands. This is an extension of #35. 3 4 5 6 looks appealing because those all look like good, low cards, but they don't make good low hands. All of the things that are bad about playing 2 3 4 5 are all the worse when playing 3 4 5 6 and above.

37. One-gap hands have a weakness that must be addressed. That is, you need exactly one specific card to give you a straight draw, and that's always a longshot draw before the flop. If you hold four of the top five cards (A K Q J T) you will always need the fifth card to appear on the board to have the nut straight. This is not to say that these hands are unplayable. As long as you have other draws, they are actually good hands, especially if they're suited or double suited. One-gappers are not necessarily bad hands. Just be aware that you are slightly handicapped until you see the flop. If conditions are not favorable, there's no law that says you have to play the hand anyway.

38. A 4 X X is much worse than it looks. For you to have the best low hand before the flop, no one else can have A 2, A 3 or 2 3. With nine opponents who hold fifty-four combined hands against you, the odds of that happening are about 1,000-1. Also, you need a 2 *and* a 3 to make the nuts, and the odds against that are greater than 100-1.

39. The only time you can profitably play A 4 X X (other than in the big blind) is if you hold A 4 K K or A 4 Q Q, and it obviously helps a lot if they're suited or double suited. Since your chances for low are dismal, the hand is more likely to win high if you hold the right cards. You can flop a set, make a full house, and have two high straight cards. If they are also suited, then you have the straight, the flush, and the full house draws. Not a bad hand.

40. If you play high cards and you get a good flop, you should realize that the only action you'll be getting will be from other high hands. Think ahead. If you're going to play a hand so that you can draw to a high hand, you should make sure you're drawing to the nuts. Your hand will be obvious, so you'd better have the cards to back it up.

Hand Selection Summary

It's not necessary to memorize these entire three chapters in order to have an idea of how to choose your starting Omaha hand. You'll still be a winner if you look at the big picture and keep in mind these broad, general, overall strategy guidelines:

1. Try to play hands that can scoop the pot by winning both the high and low.
2. Be sure that all four of your cards work together.
3. Draw only to the nuts.
4. Realize the importance of being suited.
5. Don't play for low without an ace.
6. Always have more than one possible draw working.

All other advice about hand selection is just another way to elaborate on the above general guidelines.

The advice you've just read in these chapters was specifically designed to be on the conservative side. The nature of winning Omaha requires that, and there's no way to get around it. It is intended to keep you out of trouble and to protect your bankroll while you're gaining experience and learning the other aspects of the game. Don't forget that only about 15% of all Omaha hands are winning hands in the long run. That means that if you're not in the blind, you should be playing about only one of every six or seven hands. You'll undoubtedly notice that the players around you will be playing a lot more hands than that, but if you're as sharp as I think you are, you'll also notice that they aren't winning.

Is it ever correct to play looser than the way I've described in this chapter? The answer — as is the case with almost any poker-related question — is "It depends." If you have a solid understanding of poker theory, you might recognize opportunities where it is correct to play a little looser. But don't forget that at the showdown, when you have to reveal your cards to claim the pot, the most important factor that you should have considered in the play of that hand was hand selection.

Final Exam

This was a lengthy chapter, and it's important that you understand its main point. Before you go on to the next chapter, I want you to take a test. This will test your ability to absorb information as a student, and it will test my ability as a teacher. You must score 100% on this test. Don't take this test unless you are well-rested, fresh, alert, and free of all other distractions. This is an open-book test. Be sure to use a #2 lead pencil, and once you begin the test, you have one hour to finish it. The answer is buried somewhere in the book. Take your time, and good luck.

Q: If I say "Omaha," you should immediately say:

A. Nebraska
B. Steaks
C. Schmomaha
D. Hand Selection

9

OUTS

One of the things that makes Omaha a fun game to play is that you will always have a lot of outs after the flop. Any time you're drawing to a straight and a flush, a low and a flush, or a flush and a full house, there will be many cards that will help your hand. What follows are examples of the common draws that you'll be seeing in an Omaha game.

Straight Draws

In no other instance is the difference between drawing to a hand in hold 'em and drawing to a hand in Omaha more striking than when drawing to a straight. In hold 'em, you either have a gutshot with four outs or you have an open-ender with eight outs. That's it. That's just the beginning in Omaha, where you can have as many as twenty outs to make a straight.

The following examples of straight draws will all use 9♦8♥ on the board when possible, and the third card will be irrelevant to the straight draws. I'm maintaining this consistency so that you can more easily compare the nine examples of straight draws that you're about to read. An X card in your hand means that card is also irrelevant to the straight draw. The odds are given in percentages; they're listed with two cards to come and then (in case you miss on the turn) with one card to come.

1.   Your hand is:

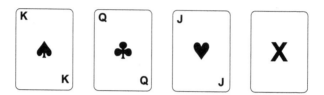

The board is:

Number of outs: 4 (T♠, T♣, T♥, T♦). Odds: 17.2%; 9.1%.

This is the worst straight draw you can have in any poker game. It's a bad draw at hold 'em, and it's even worse at Omaha. It's too easy to lose the hand after you make the straight.

2. **Your hand is:**

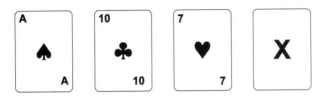

The board is:

Number of outs: 8 (J♠, J♣, J♥, J♦, 6♠, 6♣, 6♥, 6♦).
Odds: 32.7%; 18.2%.

This is the best straight draw you can have at hold 'em, but it's one of the worst at Omaha. Many veteran Omaha players will not play past the flop if this is their only draw. That's not because a straight is a bad hand or because you can't make the nuts with a straight. It's just that this is a very vulnerable hand given the large number of possible hand combinations played against it with more cards to come.

3.   Your hand is:

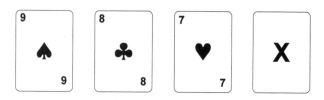

The board is:

Number of outs: 9 (9♣, 9♥, 9♦, 8♠, 8♥, 8♦, 7♠, 7♣, 7♦). Odds: 36.7%; 20.5%.

This is a three-gapper. It gives you only one more out than the open-ender. Again, you can't make the straight without giving another player a draw to a hand than can beat you.

4.   **Your hand is:**

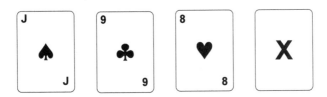

The board is:

Number of outs: 13 (J♣, J♥, J♦, 9♠, 9♥, 9♦, 8♠, 8♣, 8♦, 6♠, 6♣, 6♥, 6♦). Odds: 49.9%; 29.6%.

Having thirteen outs gives you a virtual 50% chance of making the hand after the flop. Thirteen outs is the minimum number that a lot of Omaha players require to play the hand past the flop, if two other conditions are met:

1. They are likely to win the whole high pot because no low will be possible.
2. They're drawing to the nuts.

5.   **Your hand is:**

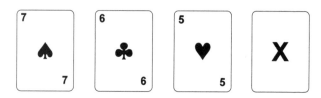

The board is:

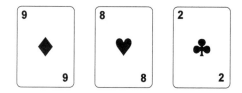

Number of outs: 13 (T♠, T♣, T♥, T♦, 7♣, 7♥, 7♦, 6♠, 6♥, 6♦, 5♠, 5♣, 5♦). Odds: 49.9%; 29.6%.

All three of your cards are lower than the board, which means that you will not have the nuts if you make the straight. This is a bad hand to try to make if that's all you have going for you.

6. **Your hand is:**

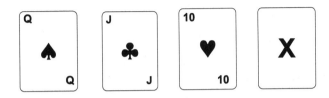

The board is:

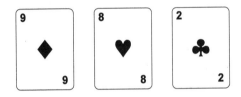

Number of outs: 13 (Q♣, Q♥, Q♦, J♠, J♥, J♦, T♠, T♣, T♦, 7♠, 7♣, 7♥, 7♦). Odds: 49.9%; 29.6%.

This hand is a hundred times better than the above hand, even though they both have the same number of outs. Why? Because all three of your cards are higher than the cards on the board, and that means you're drawing to the nuts.

7. **Your hand is:**

The board is:

Number of outs: 17 (J♠, J♣, J♥, J♦, T♣, T♥, T♦, 7♠, 7♥, 7♦, 6♠, 6♣, 6♦, 5♠, 5♣, 5♥, 5♦). Odds: 61.8%; 38.6%.

Any card from the 5 to the jack (that doesn't pair the 8 or 9 on the board) will give you the straight. This is a good hand, but be aware that a 7 or ten gives you the straight but does not make you the nuts.

8. **Your hand is:**

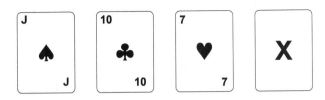

The board is:

Number of outs: 17 (Q♠, Q♣, Q♥, Q♦, J♣, J♥, J♦, T♠, T♥, T♦, 7♠, 7♣, 7♦, 6♠, 6♣, 6♥, 6♦). Odds: 61.8%; 38.6%.

Having two cards higher than the flop offers you more protection. Making the low end of the straight gives you the nuts.

9.   **Your hand is:**

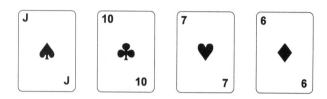

The board is:

Number of outs: 20 (Q♠, Q♣, Q♥, Q♦, J♣, J♥, J♦, T♠, T♥, T♦, 7♠, 7♣, 7♦, 6♠, 6♣, 6♥, 5♠, 5♣, 5♥, 5♦). Odds: 69.7%; 49.5%.

This is the Maine to Spain hand. Over half of the remaining deck will make your hand. If you miss on the turn, you will still make the hand one-half of the time. Only a ten will make you a straight that is not the nuts.

Flush Draws

Discounting backdoor draws, there are only two different flush draws in Omaha. The first is where you hold two flush cards in your hand and you get two more on the flop. The other is where you hold three or four flush cards in your hand and you get two more on the flop.

10. **Your hand is:**

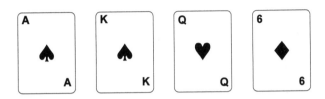

The board is:

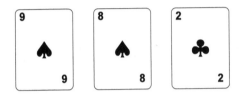

Number of outs: 9 (2♠, 3♠, 4♠, 5♠, 6♠, 7♠, T♠, J♠, Q♠).
Odds: 36.7%; 20.5%.

This is the same basic flush draw as you'd see in hold 'em.

11. **Your hand is:**

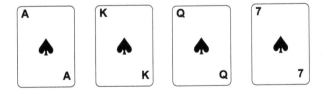

The board is:

Number of outs: 7 (2♠, 3♠, 4♠, 5♠, 6♠, T♠, J♠). Odds: 29.0%; 15.0%.

This is still your basic flush draw, but there's one important difference. You have four of the spades in your hand. You have stopped yourself, which reduces your odds of making the flush.

Low Draws

You can have two, three, or four low cards in your hand when you get two new low cards on the flop to give you a low draw.

12.   **Your hand is:**

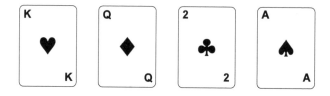

The board is:

Number of outs: 16 (8♠, 8♣, 8♥, 8♦, 7♠, 7♣, 7♥, 7♦, 6♠, 6♣, 6♥, 6♦, 5♠, 5♣, 5♥, 5♦). Odds: 59.0%; 36.7%.

In one way, this is a good hand — you have sixteen outs,

and you're drawing to the nut low. In another way, it's not a good hand — you need to get your low card and then not pair your ace or deuce on the river. That will happen only about 33% of the time. In addition, you then need to have the only A 2, so that you don't lose money by getting quartered.

13.   Your hand is:

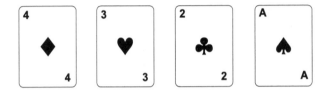

The board is:

Number of outs: 20 (6♠, 6♣, 6♥, 6♦, 5♠, 5♣, 5♥, 5♦, 4♠, 4♣, 4♥, 3♠, 3♣, 3♦, 2♠, 2♥, 2♦, A♣, A♥, A♦). Odds: 69.7%; 45.5%.

This is the best low draw you can get. Whenever you have four low cards with two new low cards on the board, you have an uncounterfeitable hand if you make the low. There are no two cards that can come that will make you the low without making you the nut low.

Straight & Flush Draws

Having both a straight and a flush draw gives you extra power. Take a look:

14. **Your hand is:**

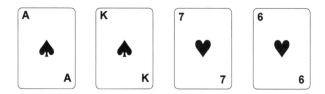

The board is:

Number of outs: 15 (Q♠, J♠, T♠, 7♠, 6♠, 5♠, 4♠, 3♠, 2♠, T♣, T♥, T♦, 5♣, 5♥, 5♦). Odds: 56.1%; 34.1%.

This hand is one of the basic, common drawing hands in Omaha, and it's all the better if you're drawing to the nuts. If you make the straight on the turn, you don't have to fear a spade on the river, because that also gives you the nuts. Making a hand with a draw to an even better hand is what it's all about in Omaha. What if you made the straight on the turn, a spade came on the river, and you didn't have the two spades in your hand? Can you see how much worse your hand would be?

Straight & Low Draws

A combined straight and low draw gives you the same kind of extra power as a combined straight and flush draw.

15. **Your hand is:**

The board is:

Number of outs: 20 (Q♠, Q♣, Q♥, Q♦, 7♠, 7♣, 7♥, 7♦, 6♠, 6♣, 6♥, 6♦, 5♠, 5♣, 5♥, 5♦, A♠, A♣, A♥, A♦). Odds: 69.7%; 45.5%.

This is one of the best draws in Omaha. You'll make one hand or the other seven out of ten times. Sometimes you'll even make both hands, which will give you a chance to scoop the whole pot.

Flush, Straight & Low Draws

16.   Your hand is:

The board is:

Number of outs: 24 (Q♠, Q♣, Q♥, Q♦, 7♠, 7♣, 7♥, 7♦, 6♠, 6♣, 6♥, 6♦, 5♠, 5♣, 5♥, 5♦, A♠, A♣, A♥, A♦, 2♥, 3♥, 4♥, K♥). Odds: 78.8%; 54.5%.

This is a great hand, but it's very hard to come by. In a 10-handed game you'll be facing this kind of hand nine times as often as you will have the hand yourself. This hand shows why you always need to be drawing to the nuts in Omaha (if you're not, someone else is).

Two Pair & Straight Draws

17.   **Your hand is:**

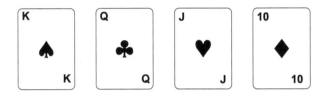

The board is:

Number of outs: 12 (A♠, A♣, A♥, A♦, K♣, K♥, Q♠, Q♦, 9♠, 9♣, 9♥, 9♦). Odds: 46.7%; 27.3%.

You don't have as many outs as you did with a flush draw, but you are drawing to the nut straight. Plus, if you make the full house, it will probably be the nuts.

Trips, Straight & Flush Draws

18. **Your hand is:**

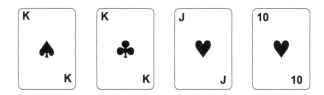

The board is:

Number of outs: 21 (A♠, A♣, A♥, A♦, K♦, Q♣, Q♠, Q♦, 9♠, 9♣, 9♥, 9♦, 2♠, 2♥, 2♦, 8♥, 7♥, 6♥, 5♥, 4♥, 3♥). Odds: 72.1%; 47.7%.

With trips, your hand can improve in many ways. If you have a pair (as you do here), a third of your rank and a pair on the board will make you a full house. That's six outs here. A pair on the board that matches the one in your hand gives you four-of-a-kind, and that's another out here. In this example, your hand can also improve to a straight (8 more outs) or a flush (6 more outs).

Straight, Flush, Full House & Low Draws

19. **Your hand is:**

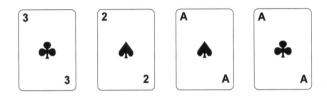

The board is:

Number of outs: 28 (A♥, 5♣, 5♥, 5♦, 9♣, 9♥, 9♦, 3♠, 4♠, 6♠, 7♠, 8♠, T♠, J♠, Q♠, K♠, 4♣, 4♥, 4♦, 6♣, 6♥, 6♦, 7♣, 7♥, 7♦, 8♣, 8♥, 8♦). Odds: 86.3%; 63.6%.

This is the dream hand. A A 2 3 double suited is the best starting hand in Omaha hi-low split. You will be dealt this hand only once every 2,820 hands. It will be suited only once every 4,028 times and double suited only once every 20,142 times.

Typical Omaha Hand

20.   **Your hand is:**

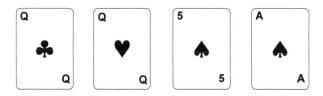

The board is:

You have flopped the nut flush draw with a mediocre low draw and an overpair. Your outs at this point are:

Flush: 8♠, T♠, J♠, K♠
Flush & Trips: Q♠
Flush & Low: 3♠, 4♠, 6♠, 7♠
Trips Only: Q♦
Low Only: 3♣, 3♥, 3♦, 4♣, 4♥, 4♦, 6♣, 6♥, 6♦, 7♣, 7♥, 7♦, 7♣, 7♥

This gives you twenty-four outs to make your hand; however, only the nine spades will give you the nuts. Look at all of the other hands that your opponents could be playing against you:

1. A♥Q♦9♦9♣. This player has flopped top set on the board. If the board pairs, your flush cannot win.

2. K♥Q♠J♣T♥. This player has the high end of the straight draw. Any 7, T, J, Q, or K will give him the nut straight. Any ♥ on the turn will also give him a flush draw.

3. 4♥6♥7♥8♠. This player has the low end of the straight draw, as well as a low draw. An ace on the turn will counterfeit your low draw and give this player a A 2 4 6 8 low.

4. A♣3♣4♠7♦. This player has the nut low draw. Any new low card besides an ace or a 3 will give him the nuts. The only way you can beat this player for low is by getting exactly a 3 and a 4 on the turn and river.

5. 3♦4♣5♥6♠. This player probably thought he started with a very good low hand. The problem is that he needs exactly an ace on the turn, and the odds of getting it are 9-1 against. And then it's very likely that he'll get quartered.

6. J♥J♠T♠T♦. This player has the high end of the straight draw — only a queen or a 7 will make his hand. He also has a flush draw, but it is only jack-high. Recall my earlier advice about not trying to make a third-highest flush. This is why. Many players would not call with the open-end straight draw because of the chance of losing to a higher straight on the river.

This hand does have some added equity, however. This player is taking four of the eight tens and jacks out of the hands of his opponents, which means that any other player is slightly less likely to be holding both the jack and the ten that he needs to make the higher straight to win on the river. This player also has a 9% chance of making three jacks or three tens on the turn, which would give him a full house draw on the river.

7. 2♣2♥6♦7♣. This player has bottom set and the low end of the straight draw. If he makes a low hand, he practically can't win low because almost any two low cards will beat him.

You might have heard it mentioned before that it's often a good idea to fold on the flop in Omaha if all you have is bottom set. If you're a typical hold 'em player, this advice probably sounded preposterous to you. It's almost unheard of for a hold 'em player to play a pocket pair and then throw his hand away when he makes the set on the flop.

As your fellow hold 'em player, I'd like to explain to you why throwing a low set away is good advice for an Omaha player. I had a hard time believing and understanding that advice myself when I first heard it, but I have since come to realize that it's advice well worth heeding under the correct circumstances.

Of all of the bits of advice I've heard about how to play Omaha, this is the one that was the hardest for me to swallow. To help make the reasoning behind this advice more clear, let me ask you some questions about hold 'em:

1. If you were drawing to a flush and the board were paired, what would you say your chances of winning the hand were? 3-1? 10-1? 20-1? How bad would the odds have to be for you to fold the hand?

2. If you have a gutshot straight draw on the flop and you miss on the turn, your odds of hitting the inside straight on the river are 10-1. Do you usually fold on the turn because of the high odds against making the hand?

3. If you hold 6♣6♥ and the flop is A♠K♠8♥, do you call, trying to hit a 6 on the turn, even though the odds against it are 22-1?

4. If the flop is Q♥T♥T♦, do you call with 7♦4♦, trying to hit the 22-1 backdoor flush? (Of course not.)

For a hold 'em player, folding all of the above-mentioned hands makes sense. You're getting terrible odds to make each hand and further reduced odds of winning if you do make the hand. To be able to fold bottom set in Omaha, you have to believe that someone has a higher set than you do.

If someone does have a higher set (which is easy in Omaha), all you have to do is realize that there's only one other card in the deck that will help you, and the odds of getting it are 44-1 against. You wouldn't play a hold 'em hand when the odds are 44-1 against you, would you? I can tell you that it doesn't make any difference if the game is Omaha.

8. 3♥3♠4♦5♦. This is another hand that looks good for low but usually doesn't win. You need exactly an ace and a deuce to make the nuts.

9. A♦6♣7♠8♣. This hand can also make a low, but anyone holding 3 4, 3 5, 3 6, 4 5, 4 6, or 5 6 will beat this player. There is a strategy that some bad players will use to try to win low with bad cards, but I don't recommend it. They believe you should play any two low cards, even if they're bad, and hope that either you're the only player in the game going low or that no other player will call with a bad low hand. I've seen players try this strategy. They do win once in a great while, but it's a losing way to play.

Final Comment about Outs

The purpose of this chapter was to get you to think about outs, both yours and your opponents'. There wasn't any exceedingly difficult material here for you to learn. The main point was to let you see the cards that will help your common draws and make you realize that you will always have more outs to draw to in Omaha than you would in hold 'em.

There is, however, one very important question still unanswered in this chapter, and only you can answer it. The question is, "How many outs do you personally need to justify playing past the flop?" Highly skilled and professional Omaha players have already answered this question in advance, and you should, too. Most players agree that they will fold the hand on the flop if they have only two, four or six outs. Most good Omaha players also usually fold if they have only eight outs, as with the open-end straight draw. Would you play if you had only nine outs, as with the flush draw? Or do you require thirteen (or even seventeen) outs to continue past the flop? Only you can answer this question.

To help you make your decision, here's a bit more advice:

1. The better the pot odds are, the fewer outs you can live with.
2. Fewer outs are okay if you're drawing to the nuts.

Good luck!

10

TOURNAMENTS

One way that the average low limit Omaha player can score a big win and really increase his hourly rate (other than hitting a jackpot) is by winning or placing high in an Omaha tournament. If you're in a tournament you can sometimes win more than $1,000 for just three hours of play. Even if you're not planning to play in tournaments, learning tournament strategy can be very valuable to you because it speeds up your learning process and helps you play better in your regular ring (full, non-tournament) game.

There is a big difference between tournament and ring game strategy. The difference is so great that a player who is a good player in his regular ring game will almost never win a tournament if he uses just his ring game strategies throughout the tournament. Although the subject of tournament strategy is so vast that it's more properly addressed in a separate book, I'd like to take the time to give you some of the more important points.

Top 41 Tournament Tips
1. Should you play in a particular Omaha tournament? I play tournaments. I use two criteria to answer that ques-

tion. Either I have to believe that I have a reasonable chance to make the final table (get in the money), or I must think that the tournament practice and experience I will get by entering this tournament will be worth the entry fee. There are many good tournaments with $5-$20 entry fees that are worth the experience.

2. Before you play any tournament, make sure you know all of the rules and conditions. How much is the initial buy-in? How much are rebuys? When can you rebuy? In some tournaments you can't rebuy unless you're below your initial buy-in. How much is the add-on, and when can you make it? How many players will be at each table? How many tables will there be? What is the estimated total payout, and how is it structured? Are the players allowed to make a deal at the final table? Will there be pictures taken or an award ceremony after the tournament?

3. You must determine if the tournament is designed to be fast, slow, or somewhere in between. The three factors you look at to do this are:

1. The amount of chips you start with.
2. The initial betting limit.
3. The time length of each round.

The first thing you do is determine the ratio of total chips to the size of the big bet. Ideally, you'd like this to be 15-1 or more. Some tournaments start with $200 in chips and a $10-$20 betting limit, which is a ratio of 10-1. In a scenario like that, you could possibly lose all of your chips in the first hand (and I have). As you can see, a low ratio means a fast tournament. If the length of each betting stage is fifteen or twenty minutes, that also makes for a fast tournament. A ratio of 15-1 or higher with stages of more than twenty minutes makes for a slower tournament.

How does knowing all this help you? The main purpose of a tournament is to get poker players into the poker room on that room's slower days. The poker room hopes that players will bust out of the tournament and then take seats in ring games that can be raked. This practice obviously creates business for the room when there might otherwise not be a game there that day. Knowing if the tournament is designed to be fast or slow tells you what the mix of luck and skill will be and what the chances are that you'll make the final table.

Obviously, good players will beat bad players in the long run. However, bad and lucky players can and do beat good players in the short run. The best weapon that good players have against bad players is time. The longer each stage of the tournament is, the better the odds are for the better players. A tournament with a small betting ratio and short time limits is almost like a crap shoot. Anyone can win. If you're a good player, you should look for the slower tournaments.

4. The number-one difference between a ring game and a tournament is that in a tournament, survival is what it's all about. In a ring game, you can consistently play inferior hands voluntarily, because you can lose five hands in a row

and then make it all back on the sixth hand. And if you run out of poker chips before you win that sixth hand, you can always buy more. You can't play inferior hands in a tournament. One or two hands could take all of your chips, and you cannot buy any more.

5. Any game or tournament will always have a mix of good and bad players; however, the skill level of the players in tournaments is almost always much higher than the skill level of players in a typical ring game. This is a double-edged sword. It's more difficult to beat better players; yet in a tournament they are easier to read and more predictable than the bad players.

6. If you're playing in a tournament that allows rebuys and add-ons, you should be prepared to make the maximum number of rebuys and add-ons. Tournaments like this are as much a contest to see who can buy the most chips as they are a contest to win those chips. You need to be able to keep up with the competition just to have a chance to make the final table. You can play a little faster earlier because of the rebuys and add-ons.

7. If you're going to make a rebuy and/or an add-on, there are two questions you must answer before doing so:

1. *Why* did I lose all of my chips?
If you were unlucky or just failed to make routine draws then you should go ahead and make the rebuy. If you lost because you were outplayed and because you're facing su-perior-quality competition, then you should consider not

making the rebuy.

2. *Who* has most of the chips at my table?
If the answer is "the good players," you should realize that your chances of making the final table just got worse. You should consider not making the rebuy.

8. If you're free to make the rebuy and add-on at any time, you should consider waiting as long as possible to do so. A short-term run of bad luck can wipe out your stack before your skill has a chance to kick in and take effect. It's better to go **all-in** with what you have, lose, and then make the rebuy. Going all-in will cut your losses when you lose the hand, and you will still have the rebuy option available to you.

Some players like to have as many chips in front of them as possible. Their reasoning is: "When I make my hand I want to be able to play it all the way and get maximum value from it." That's a good ring game strategy, but it's a bad tournament strategy. It's a very bad idea to push small, statistical advantages and edges in a tournament. It's a high standard deviation strategy, and you can have negative swings big enough to knock yourself out of the tournament. If anything, save your rebuy and add-on so you can lose it later rather than earlier. (And since only one player can win the tournament, this is what will happen anyway.)

9. During the first hour of the tournament, you should be watching all of your opponents closely to determine their skill levels, playing styles, levels of patience, playing patterns, personalities and availability of tells. If you don't want to do all of this work, or if you don't see the value in it, you should at least pay attention to the cards that the players turn up at the end of the hand. With that information, you can make judgments about their skills and knowledge of position and hand selection. I guarantee you that the players who will make the final table are already doing this to you.

10. Each player's stack size is of paramount importance in a tournament. You should not ordinarily attack a bigger stack than yours. You could be eliminated from the tournament if you lose the hand, while your opponents will only lose some chips to you and will remain in the tournament.

11. If it is a rebuy event, you can and should play a little more liberally during the rebuy period. You can afford to take chances in an effort to get ahead, and losing won't bust you out of the tournament.

12. Alternatively, you might already be a great tournament player, and you want your image to be that of a Tight-Aggressive player. In that case, you should play super-tight and "by the book." This will discourage other players from playing when you're in the pot, which will in turn increase your chance of winning the hands you do play. You won't be bluffed as often. You will be able to check down more hands, and you might be able to bluff a little more often because of your image.

Not one of these benefits of playing tight is the major reason for playing tight, however. The number-one reason you want to have a super tight image throughout the tournament is so that you can change gears in the later stages of the tournament (when the limits are higher and mistakes are more deadly) and your opponents won't know it until they lose a big pot to you because they misread your hand. I promise you that the eventual winner of the next tournament you play in will do this to you, so you might as well learn how to do it also.

13. Decide ahead of time exactly which hands you will play and under what circumstances. Decide which hands you will use to call pre-flop raises.

14. Always be aware of your position relative to the button. This will help you decide if another player is making a move based more on his position than his cards.

15. Always be aware of the other players' stack sizes, especially before the play of the hand. Players with small stacks are usually more reluctant to call your bets and raises if you act before they do on the hand.

16. If you are short-stacked, the time to make a move is before you are reduced to about four times the combined amount of the blinds. Most players wait too long to make this move because they are just trying to survive. If the blinds are $50-$100 then you should not let your stack get below $600 — ($50 + $100) x 4 — before you take a stand with a hand. Taking your stand earlier gives you the freedom to play the hand correctly and get maximum value without taking extra risks.

17. Always be aware of how much time is left in the current stage of the tournament. Certain strategies become more effective near the end of each stage.

18. Always have an idea of how much the blinds and the antes will cost you to play each round. Use this to determine how many hands you have before you will be blinded out if you don't win a hand or make a move.

19. Pay attention to the cost of calling the rest of the small blind. Most of the time the correct play is to fold. Learn not to over-defend your big blind. Even extremely high pot odds can't turn a losing hand into a winning hand.

20. When an opponent plays a hand, and he is not in one of the blinds, you need to determine why he is playing that hand. Sometimes the reason will be obvious. He might be a bad player, he might be short-stacked or he might be in good position. Whatever it is, you need to know why playing that hand makes sense to him. This will help you read his hand and avoid mistakes when playing against him. Both of these factors contribute to your overall goal, which is not to lose any chips

21. The same thing applies when you play a hand and you're not in the blind. You had better know exactly why you're playing the hand, because if you haven't given it any thought, someone playing against you already has.

22. Keep in mind that you cannot win a tournament before the half-time break, but you can lose it by then. Your job in the first half is mainly just to survive and put yourself in good position to begin the second half.

23. Tighten up considerably after the rebuy period ends. You're playing for keeps now. You cannot replace the chips you lose except by winning them back from the other players.

24. Never miss an opportunity to put a player all-in. If an opponent bets ten of his eleven chips, and you have forty-five chips, you should always raise one more to get him all-in. You've probably heard the saying that all a player needs to beat you is a chip and a chair. It's true. Try to deprive him of both.

25. Learn to gang up on all-in players, especially at the final table. If one player is all-in and is called by another player, with any reasonable hand, you should also call (if you don't fear a raise). All of the players with chips should then check the hand all the way to the river in an effort to increase the odds that one of them will beat (and therefore knock out of the tournament) the all-in player. Similarly, you should bet only if you have the nuts on the river. This helps all of you because the objective in a tournament is not to win pots, but to move up the payout ladder.

26. Do not underestimate the value of a single chip. Do not play too loose, wild or reckless in the beginning of the tournament, just because you have a lot of chips and the limits are small. This is one of the more common mistakes that beginning players make. Do not confuse it with playing fast, which is often correct. Playing fast means betting and raising at every reasonable opportunity, rather than playing a little more conservatively.

27. Be aware of how many total chips are in play in the tournament and of how many players there are left. With this information, you'll be able to determine the average number of chips for each player.

28. If you have a small stack late in the tournament, you must realize that you will probably not win the tournament. Your goal, therefore, is to move up the payout ladder as best you can. Look at the other players' stacks and give those players every chance to bust each other out before you get blinded out.

29. Throwing away A♣A♥ or K♦K♠ before the flop can be profitable, especially at the final table. As an example, let's look at a scenario.

Imagine you're in a tournament. There are five of you left, and the payouts are:

1st - $4,000
2nd - $2,000
3rd - $1,000
4th - $500
5th - $300

TOURNAMENTS

The chips are distributed as follows:
Carissa - 30,000
Jim - 2,000
Neil - 2,000
Sherry - 2,000
You - 500

At least you made the final table, so you're getting at least $300 in prize money. You get your hand, and Sherry raises to 2,000 all-in, Neil calls all-in, Jim calls all-in, and Carissa calls, which leaves her with 28,000 chips. You look at your hand, and you have A♣A♥! What do you do?

If you call and win the hand, you will have 2,500 chips. If you lose the hand, you'll be busted out, and you'll receive $300. If you fold, you're guaranteed to move up the pay ladder, no matter what happens after that. In the very unlikely event of a tie, two of the players with only 2,000 chips will be eliminated, and, quite possibly, all three will lose to Carissa. This means you'd move up two (or even three) places by not playing the hand.

If Carissa wins the hand, your payout goes from $300 to a guaranteed minimum of $2,000. If she does not win the hand, she will have 28,000 chips, and the winner of the hand will have 6,000 chips. Then this line of logic starts all over again. If you can stay out of the way while she knocks off the other player, you then get second place for sure.

This example is extreme and unlikely, but I made it that

way to illustrate the point more clearly. The situation described above will probably never happen to you, but understanding the logic is what's valuable to you. You'll often be in a spot where you'll be telling yourself, "I'm not going to play this (usually playable) great hand because all I need to do is sit back and wait for one player to bust out another player." Or, "I don't need to play this hand (knowing that I could bust someone out) because I can already see that another player is going to do that for me."

Here's the fundamental truth about winning tournaments: it's about moving up the pay ladder, not necessarily about winning pots. Believe it or not, it is possible to come in second place in a tournament without ever winning a single hand.

30. If you're short stacked, try to survive your big and small blind by not calling in the small blind or by not playing after the flop. This might give you as many as eight more hands to look at before you get blinded out.

31. The IRS requires casinos to issue a Form WG-2 to anyone in the tournament who receives $600 or more. If you're making a deal at the final table and you don't want a WG-2, you can ask for $599 or less and avoid the IRS paperwork.

32. A player who is eager to make a deal at the last table will probably play more conservatively than usual if his offer to make a deal is refused. After all, he did just tell you that he doesn't want to put any more money at risk.

33. It's never too late to make a deal. As soon as you realize you're in chip trouble or you're facing elimination, you should try to make a deal. You have a lot to gain and nothing to lose.

34. Traditionally, tournament players are not allowed to select a table or a seat at that table. However, there are a few poker rooms that allow it, even though it may not be well known. Ask if you can choose your own seat and table. If you can, get a seat at what you know will be the final table. That way, you will be one of the few players in the tournament who isn't forcibly moved from table to table. You might avoid paying double blinds and being in bad position.

35. If you can choose your own seat at the table, you should choose the 3rd or the 8th seat, because all of the players will be in your field of vision at the same time. Seeing everyone at once will help you pick up tells and gather all the information you need to make your decisions. If the 3rd or 8th seat is not available, then the seats on either side of them will serve equally well.

36. Watch the best tournament player at your table, especially early in the tournament. Stay out of his way unless you have great cards.

37. If you bust out of the tournament before making the final table, you should stay around to watch the play at the final table. Not only will the winner of the tournament unwittingly give you lessons, you'll also know who are the good tournament players. Do this often enough and you'll be able to recognize these players at the beginning of future tournaments.

38. Find out how long it takes to play a tournament down to the final table. Then compute how much each place is worth. Use this information to calculate how much each tournament is worth to you per hour (assuming you get in the money) and convert that number to the number of big bets per hour, using the size of the big bet in the game you usually play. You can then use this information to compare the potential worth of various tournaments and ring games.

The tournament advice you just read is designed for and applies to almost any poker tournament, especially Texas hold 'em tournaments. If you understand the fundamentals of tournament strategy and recognize how tournaments differ from regular ring games, you will do well in any tournament. Here are a few more points that apply only to Omaha hi-low split:

39. Consider limping in with big hands like A A 2 3, A A 2 4 or A A K K. You should not mind occasionally trying to win more than the blinds.

40. High hands gain value later in the tournament because the low hands (correctly) don't want to draw to their lows. It's the same as playing a straight or flush draw. You're going to miss two out of three times, and that's too much to give away in the late stages of a tournament.

TOURNAMENTS

41. Don't play for low when it's two- or three-handed. You will miss too often, and you will win very little when you do make the hand. Winning one-half of the pot one-third of the time is a sure-fire way to give away your money.

I have one final thought about tournaments. If you're new to Omaha, and you've decided that you're going to do what it takes to be a better player, then you've probably decided to set aside a certain amount of time and money to accomplish this goal. You've decided that you're willing to make an investment in the game, knowing that it will pay dividends for you in the future.

I want you to know that in this situation, dollar for dollar, the experience you will get from tournaments will be more valuable to you than the same amount of time and money spent playing in a ring game. If you have, for example, $100 to invest in learning the game, you will get the most for your dollar if you can play in several small buy-in tournaments rather than taking a seat in a ring game with that $100. If anything, you'll see that you pay closer attention and learn a lot faster when you're faced with the possibility of being busted out of the game if you lose. Good luck!

11

OMAHA AND THE INTERNET

A 2002 survey of 10,000 high school English teachers nationwide revealed that a majority of those teachers thought it was more important for high school students to learn how to navigate the Internet than it was for them to learn Shakespeare. My, how the world has changed.

Modern poker has been around for about one-hundred-and-fifty years only. While it has evolved, and different games have come into existence, certain aspects of the game have always remained the same. To play poker, for example, you've always had to physically travel to get to the game, or, if the game was at your place, the other players have had to come to you. You've traditionally had to have cold, hard cash to play, and if you were a winner, you always took your winnings with you when the game was over.

The biggest change in poker today is not in the game itself but rather in its availability and accessibility. Due to the explosion of the Internet in the past ten years, there are now thousands of Internet casinos and hundreds of other sites where you can play poker. The volume of money put into action through online gambling is second only to the amount of money involved in Internet "adult entertainment" sites. Well, I guess in one way the world hasn't changed that much after all.

If you're a poker player and you want to play over the Internet, there are only two major categories of information that you need to know about. First, you should know about Internet casinos. Second, you should know about websites dedicated only to poker.

This book is about how to play Omaha. It's not about how to gamble on the Internet. For that reason, I will not delve into the intricacies of surfing the web in search of a place to gamble. Rather, I will give you the basic information you need to know just so you can stay up-to-date with your poker-playing friends.

Internet Casinos

There are some very good reasons why there are so many Internet casinos and why so many people like to gamble over the Internet. The most attractive features have universal appeal. All you need to play is a computer, an Internet connection, and a means of depositing funds in your account.

Since you can play from home, you have total privacy. You don't have to dress up to leave the house, you can play anytime (even around the clock), playing is very convenient because you don't have transportation issues, you can do it by yourself, you don't have to wait for anyone else, you have an incredible choice of different games and limits, and you can quit any time.

On the other hand, you'll have to give up some information about yourself. For you privacy buffs, the news is good. The only thing an Internet casino will know about you is your e-mail address and the small amount of technical information your Internet provider delivers with any e-mail you send. You will be asked to provide a name to go by when you play against other players at a poker table, but it can be any real or fictitious name you choose.

You can get a list of the many online casinos at www.wheretobet.com or www.internet-commission.com. There are some things you should know before you choose an Internet casino and send away any of your money. Let's take a moment to run through them.

All Internet casinos operate from outside the geographical and legal borders of the United States. Most of them are located in the Caribbean Islands. That's because current U.S. federal law prohibits this kind of gambling activity and the use of interstate communications to place and collect on these types of bets. Currently, all Internet casinos (and the attendant gambling) are legal in the United States as long as the casino is offshore.

Because of this rule, you won't have all of the safeguards that you are accustomed to when doing business with a company or a "brick and mortar" casino within the United States. There is no government body, council, oversight committee, or watchdog agency overseeing or monitoring the activities, standards, or honesty of any of these Internet casinos. That old saying, "Let the buyer beware," certainly applies in this case. However, the news is not all bad.

Despite the absence of government regulation, most Internet casinos offer you quite a good experience and are scrupulously honest. Why? It's because they are in business to make money. Like every other good businessman, they know that a long-term, mutually satisfying relationship with a customer is the best way to make the most money in the long run. The very best recommendation that an online casino can have for itself is simply the fact that it has been in business for a long time. The casino managers know that they have a lot of competition and that they are in a "word of mouth" driven business. The longer a casino has been around, the more you can be sure that they are honest, they give the player a fair shake, and they are customer-service oriented.

If you find a casino site where you think you'd like to play, there are a couple of things you should do first. Check the site to see how long it's been in business. Ask your friends (you know which ones) about their online experiences and what they do or don't recommend. Look for the 24/7 customer service toll-free phone number and/or the customer service e-mail address. Call the phone number and see if you can talk to a live person. But before you do that, check with your phone company to make sure you know in advance how much the per-minute charges will be. Send an e-mail to them and tell them that they are being tested to see how fast they can answer your e-mail. Look out for the phrase "For Personal Rather Than Professional Play" or variations thereof. That's a disclaimer in disguise. It's their way of telling you that their odds are so bad that you will never win.

Competition among online casinos is fierce. Be aware that if you sign on with an Internet casino, you will soon begin receiving unsolicited e-mail advertisements from similar sites. Some people call it junk mail.

Once you decide to play at an online casino, the next thing you need to know is that almost any computer will do except for the very oldest ones. There are three ways to play online:

1. You can download the entire casino package onto your hard drive. The disadvantage is that it initially takes a long time — up to thirty minutes. After that, everything is an advantage, because downloading provides you with superior animation, graphics, and sound. The download is permanent, and you can play any time.

2. You can use the JAVA format, which runs through your computer's browser. This saves time but sacrifices the quality of the sound and graphics.

3. You can use HTML. The biggest advantage is the speed and immediate availability of the games you want to play.

Once you actually get into a casino site, you will see that you will get to play for free with worthless, imaginary money. Casinos give you this opportunity so you can become familiar with their sites and try out the games with no risk. After you lose all of your free stake, or you've played for a certain amount of time, you will be asked if you want to deposit real money in an account.

To play for real, you have to have real money in an account with the casino. This is decision time. If you decide to go ahead, you have a variety of ways that you can get your money to the casino:

1. You can send a personal check; however, you have to wait for the check to clear before the funds will be made available to you.

2. You can send a money order; however, you also have to wait for that to clear.

3. You can send a cashier's check. Some casinos will credit your account immediately, and some will make you wait until it clears.

4. You can use your credit card. The transfer of funds is instantaneous. This isn't always an option, since one major credit card company recently took themselves out of the send-cash-to-on-line-casinos business.

Note to the extra cautious: If a site advertises that it uses a secure server to transfer funds, the use of a credit card is completely safe. There is no way that anyone else can acquire, use, or abuse your credit card information. They're using the same type of secure encryption technology that major banking institutions and governments worldwide use to transfer billions and billions of dollars every day.

5. You can send money through Western Union — that's universally accepted.

6. You can use Pay Pal or a similar secure method.

Once your money is on deposit with the casino, you will be given an account number and a password to access your account. I recommend that you open your account with a small amount of money, perhaps $50 or $100. You should play at the small limits until you're comfortable and you feel like you know what you're doing. Then you should request that a small amount of the money in your account be returned to you. The purpose of this exercise is to test their procedures and to see how long it takes to get a refund (and if you get one).

You should also keep a record or ledger of your online gambling, to protect against some sort of system failure or other problem. If there's a dispute, you are more credible if you have a record and you can definitively state which days you've played, how much you won or lost, and especially what your current balance is.

Only after you've gone through the above suggestions do I recommend that you get more deeply involved with an Internet casino. Shop around. There are a lot of excellent sites to be enjoyed, and again, word of mouth is the best advertisement. Good luck.

Internet Poker Rooms

Internet sites that are dedicated exclusively to poker are, on average, safer, better quality, and a lot more fun to play at than poker rooms that are accessed through online casinos. You should always exercise judgment and prudence when you do business over the Internet; however, I can tell you that the dangers and possible problems associated with Internet casinos are far less when you play at the best Internet poker rooms. The ones that I like are:

PlanetPoker.com
acrpoker.com
PokerStars.com
sunrise-poker.com
partypoker.com
ParadisePoker.com
ultimatebet.com
pokerroom.com

These aren't the only Internet poker rooms in existence. They're just the ones that are, in my opinion, the best of the best. Unless you have two computers with two different e-mail addresses (in which case you'd be cheating), you can play in only one game at a time anyway. These eight poker rooms offer all of the different games, limits, tournaments, and options that you could ever hope for in a poker game.

Some of the best features and advantages of playing poker

online are:

1. You can open an account with as little as $5.00!

2. Many poker rooms will add a 25% bonus to your initial buy-in if you are a first-time customer. Some poker rooms will give you up to $100 (in real money) when you open an account, regardless of your initial buy-in.

3. You can play 10¢-25¢ limit or 25¢-50¢ limit.

4. The quality of the live support and service through e-mail is superior. Many of these poker rooms are endorsed by well-known, world-class players. These rooms don't have any problems to speak of, because these players' reputations are on the line.

5. The rake is much, much lower than in a live game in a brick-and-mortar casino.

6. An online poker room is a great place to play tournaments. There are tournaments starting every hour of the day, the entry fees are low, some are freeroll tournaments, and you can play any game you want. Some tournaments pay up to fifty or even 100 places.

7. There are a lot of satellite tournaments. You can parlay a small buy-in into a poker cruise or a tournament with a $1,000,000 guaranteed prize pool.

8. Many poker rooms have free hourly cash give-aways

and other promotions.

9. You have the option to **straddle** (raise in the dark after the big blind), **play the overs** (play at a higher limit when others agree to do so), or play in kill or half-kill games.

10. You have the option to **chop** (agree with the other blind to end the hand early and take back your money), although that doesn't happen very often. It seems that the games are so loose that it's never just the blinds in the hands.

11. You can sometimes request a computer-generated profile of the playing habits of your opponents — there's an option that amazes me!

12. A few of these poker rooms also offer you the services of a sports book while you're playing poker.

The website pokerprop.com will tell you how you can earn $12-an-hour playing poker online. What a country! (Wherever it may be.)

I think playing poker online is the wave of the future. Just like the automobile replaced the horse-and-buggy, the passenger airplane replaced the dirigible, and the word processor replaced the typewriter, the online poker room will replace the brick-and-mortar poker room. I don't think that poker rooms currently in existence will fold up, never to be seen again, but I do think that fewer poker rooms will be built in the future than would have been without the Internet. That's just my opinion — I could be wrong.

Final Comment

Thank you for reading this far. I hope you enjoyed the book, and, more importantly, I hope that the book was of immediate, substantial help to you. Like I said in the beginning, this book is everything about Omaha that I wish I could have told myself years ago. I'd like to hear what you thought of it. Perhaps you have some ideas for future editions. If so, my personal e-mail address is kennolga@earthlink.net, and it would be a pleasure to hear from you.

Good luck!

GLOSSARY

All-In - The act of putting all the remaining chips you have in the pot, usually before the hand is over. A player who is all-in can only win that part of the pot that he was able to match, if he has the best hand at the end.

Baby - A 2, 3, 4 or 5 when playing for low or hi-low split.

Backdoor - Making a hand that you originally weren't drawing to, i.e., you hold A♣J♣ and the flop is Q♥7♣3♣, and the turn is the K♦ and the river is the 10♥, giving you the straight, even though you were originally hoping for the flush after the flop.

Backraise - A re-raise from a player who originally called, but when it was raised after he called, he decided to re-raise.

Bad Beat - To lose with a great hand, usually aces-full or better, to a player who made a longshot draw.

Bankroll - All of the money that you are willing and able, or have otherwise set aside, to put into a poker game. This money is either actually physically (or at least mentally) segregated from other money used for non-poker expenses.

Bicycle - A 5-high straight: 5 4 3 2 A

Big Blind - The biggest of two blinds in a hold 'em game; a mandatory bet posted by the player two places to the dealer's left.

Big Flop - A flop that give you almost everything you could hope for and helps your hand in more than one way. For example, you hold A♠A♣2♠3♣ and the flop is A♥4♠5♠. You have a set of aces, an uncounterfeitable wheel (the nut low), and the nut flush draw.

Blank - A card that is obviously of no help to a poker hand. Also called a brick.

Blockers - When the flop is three to a straight and you hold the open-end straight draw cards. For example, the flop is 9♥8♦7♣ and you hold T♠T♣6♥6♦. This makes a straight much less likely in your opponents' hands.

Boxed Card - A card that is accidentally turned face up during the shuffle and is then dealt to a player face up when it should be face down. It is treated as a blank piece of paper and is replaced with a new card after the deal is completed for that round.

Bluff - To bet with a hand that you're sure will lose if called.

Board - The cards that are turned face up in a hold 'em game and belong to everybody; also called community cards.

Burn or Burn Card - In community card games, the top card in the deck does not come into play after everyone is dealt their hole cards. The top card is mucked by the dealer before he deals the flop, turn, and river cards. This is done to protect everyone in the event the top card is marked or somehow known to one player while the action is in progress and everyone is waiting for that card.

Button - In casino games, a round, plastic disc with the word "Dealer" printed on each side. It moves clockwise with each new hand to indicate who holds the dealer's position.

Cards Speak - The concept that your poker hand is determined by what your cards actually are, and not by any remarks that a player may make about his hand. All casino poker games are played 'cards speak' and if you turn your hand face up at the end of the hand, the dealer will read the hand for you.

Carvee - A player who is being carved up. For example, on the river Player A has the wheel for the nut low. Player B has the nut full house for high. Player C has what he thinks is a good hand but he does not have the nuts in either direction. When Player C calls the maximum number of bets and raises and does not win any of the pot, he will have been carved up by Players A and B, and is therefore the carvee.

Case Card - The last card of a particular rank that has not been seen during the play of the hand or is otherwise believed to be still in the deck.

Check-raise - Not to bet initially on a round, and then to raise when the action returns to you.

Chop - When everyone but the two blinds folds, an agreement they make to take back their money and end the hand before the flop, thus avoiding the rake.

Cold Call - To call two or more bets at once as opposed to calling one bet and then calling another on the same round.

Community Cards - See **Board**.

Completed Hand - A poker hand that requires all five cards to make the hand. That would be a straight, a flush, a full house, 4 of a kind, and a straight flush.

Counterfeited - To have a made low hand and then have one of the low cards in your hand pair on the board on the river. For example, you hold A♦K♥9♦2♥, the board is 3♥6♥8♣J♠ and the river is the 2♣.

Dangler - The one card in your four-card Omaha hand

that is not coordinated with the other three cards. For example, it your hand is A♥K♥K♣7♠ , the 7♠ is the dangler. It's like playing with only three cards.

Dominated Hand - A hand that nearly always loses when competing against another particular hand. Whenever two hold 'em hands contain a common card, the hand with the higher other card dominates the other. For example, A♥K♣ dominates hands like A♠2♦ and K♥5♣.

Double Belly Buster - A straight draw that has eight outs yet it is not an open-end straight draw. For example, you have 8♦6♦ and the board is 10♥7♠4♦3♣ with one card to come. A 5 or a 9 will complete your straight.

Drawing Dead - Attempting to make a particular poker hand that, even if you make it, is already beaten or cannot possibly win.

Early Position - To be in the first third of the players in a hold 'em game to have to act on their hands.

End - See **River**.

8 or Better - When playing for low, the stipulation that your fifth highest card must be an 8 or lower to qualify as a low poker hand.

Emergency Low - A made low hand that you weren't trying to make, that you may not realize you have and certainly would not bet on if you knew you did have it.

For example, you hold A♦K♥Q♦8♥ and the board is 7♦T♣5♦2♦, giving you the nut flush. When the board pairs on the river and your sole opponent shows you his K♦J♣T♦T♥ to make a full house, you start to throw your hand away while not believing your bad luck. But wait! You also have A♦8♥ to go with the three low cards on the board to make an **emergency low** to get half of the pot.

Flop - The first three community cards placed face up by the dealer.

Flop a Set - To have a pair in the pocket and to get one more of that rank on the flop to make three of a kind; also called trips.

Flush Card - A card of the suit that you need to make your flush or to pick up a flush draw.

Flush Draw - To have four cards to a flush with one or more cards to come.

Free Card - A card received on a betting round where there turned out to be no betting on that round because everyone checked.

Freeroll - Whenever you have the nuts with more cards to come and you also have a draw to a better hand.

Full - Used to describe full houses. Whatever your three-of-a-kind is what you are full of, e.g., 8 8 8 5 5 is "8s full of 5s."

GLOSSARY

Gutshot - An inside straight draw, i.e., you hold A♦K♥ and the flop is J♣10♠7♥.

Implied Odds - Money that is not yet in the pot but you believe will be in the pot after you make your hand. It is an educated guess of what your pot odds will be when the hand is over.

High Wrap - When you have a straight draw and all four of your hole cards are higher than the cards on the board. For example, the flop is 3♠8♣9♥ and you hold T♦J♠Q♣K♥. A 7, T, jack, queen, or king will make you the nut straight.

Inside Wrap - To hold the three cards in a three-gap flop. For example, the flop is A♥T♦8♦ and you hold a jack, queen and a king in your hand. Getting any one of these cards on the turn or river will give you the nut straight.

Kicker - The highest card in your hand that does not help make a straight, flush, or full house.

Kill - A game where the betting limits are increased (usually doubled) for the next hand only.

Late Position - To be one of the last third of the players in the game to have to act on your hand.

Little Blind - The smaller of the two blinds in hold 'em, posted by the first player to the dealer's left before the cards are dealt.

Low Wrap - To hold four low cards and to get three more low cards on the flop without making a pair.

Maine to Spain - Two cards on the flop that, along with the four cards in you hand, give you a six-card straight. For example, the flop is 9♦8♣2♣ and you hold 6♣7♣T♥J♥. A 5, 6, 7, T, jack or queen will give you a straight. This is a 20-out draw.

Middle Position - To be in the middle third of the players in the game to have to act on your hand; to have approximately an equal number of players before and after you in the play of the hand.

Muck - To muck your hand is to fold and throw your hand in the discard pile. The discard pile is also called the muck.

"Nut-nut" - Said by the player at the showdown who has the nut low hand and the nut high hand. This happens most often when the nut high hand is a flush. When the board has three or more cards of the same suit and a low is possible, the player holding the ace and another card of that suit along with another low card has the nuts in both directions. For example, if the board is 3♣6♣8♥J♣K♠ the player holding A♣2♣ has the nut high and low regardless what his other two cards are. Also, the deuce does not have to be a club if one of his other cards is a club.

Nuts - The best possible hand that can be made after the flop, the turn, and especially after the river.

GLOSSARY

On the Button - In flop games like Omaha and hold 'em, to be in the dealer's position and therefore last to act throughout each betting round of that game.

Outs - The number of cards that will help your hand. For example, if you have two hearts and get two more on the flop, then there are nine hearts, or nine outs that will make your flush.

Overcall - A call made after there has already been a bet and a call. The next player to call that bet is overcalling.

Overs, Playing the - An agreement among any players in the game who want to play higher limit when there are only overs players left in the hand.

Overcard - A card on the board that is higher than any of your hole cards.

Playing the Board - You cannot actually play the board in Omaha because you must use two cards in your hand. However, you can say, "Playing the board" when there is a straight on the board and you have two of those straight cards in your hand. For example, you hold A♥2♥3♣K♣ and the board is T♥J♦Q♠K♠A♣. Your A♥ and K♣ make a straight even though there's already and ace and a king on the board. This is done as a courtesy to the dealer and helps speed up the game.

Pocket - The first two cards in hold 'em and the first four cards in Omaha that you're dealt that constitute your pri-

CARDOZA PUBLISHING • WARREN

vate hand.

Pot Odds - The ratio of the amount of money in the pot compared the amount of money that it costs to call a bet. For example, if the pot contains $42 and it cost you only $3 to call, then you are getting pot odds of 14-1. If it cost $6 to call, then you are getting pot odds of 7-1.

Rainbow flop - A flop with three different suits and no pair.

Rainbow board - One card of each suit on the board and no pair after the turn card is dealt. This obviously makes a flush impossible no matter what the river card is.

River - The fifth, and last, community card in Omaha and hold 'em; also called the end.

Rock - A poker player who has a reputation for playing only premium starting hands and whose playing style is dull, boring and very low risk.

Rough - Used to describe a made low hand that is not very good, given the highest card. A player who has 8♣7♥4♣3♠A♦ would say, "I have a rough 8." See **Smooth**.

Runner-runner - Used to describe the turn and river cards when they are exactly what you needed to win, or what your opponent needed to beat you. Also called "perfect-perfect." "I flopped the nut straight but he hit

GLOSSARY

runner-runner to make his backdoor flush draw." (This is going to happen a lot in Omaha.)

Rush - The experience of having won many pots close together in a short period of time.

Semi-bluffing - Betting with a hand that, if called, probably isn't the best hand at the moment, but has a chance to improve with more cards to come.

Set - The exact situation of having a pair in the pocket and have one of those cards on the board. Holding 9♣9♥ with a board of 3♦9♠Q♣ is a set of 9s while a holding of 3♦9♣ with a board of 9♠9♥Q♣ is also three 9s, but not a set.

Scoop - To win both the high end of the pot and the low end of the pot when playing a hi-low split game.

Slowplay - To play your hand in a much weaker manner than the strength of the hand would usually call for in order to disguise that strength for a future betting round.

Smooth - Used to describe a made low hand when it is very good, given the highest card. For example, an 8 for low is not a good low hand; however, if it is 8♦4♠3♣2♥A♥, a player would say, "I have a smooth 8." See **Rough**.

Split pot - A poker game where the intention is to split the pot between the highest poker hand and the lowest poker hand. The low hand will often have to meet qualifying criteria to claim half of the pot, such as having an 8 or better for low.

Spread Limit - A betting structure that allows you to bet any amount between the preset lowest and highest amounts. The most common spread limit used for Omaha is $2-$10.

Stop Yourself - To have more than two cards of the same rank or same suit in your hand. For example, A♣3♣9♣Q♥ or J♣J♥J♦Q♣. This is undesirable because it takes cards that you need to help make your hand out of play.

Straddle - Occurs when the first player after the big blind raises in the dark; that is, before he receives his first two cards.

Straight Draw - To have four cards to a straight with one or more cards to come.

Structured Limit - A betting structure that forces you to bet only the amount specified as the small bet and the big bet. It usually is a 1:2 ratio.

Tell - A clue from an opponent that helps you figure out what his poker hand is. That clue (or clues) can be either made voluntarily or involuntarily, knowingly or unknowingly, and either verbally or with physical movement only.

Through ticket - A poker hand that you know you're going to play all the way to the river because it is either very good on the flop, or has so many outs to make, or has the potential to make a monster hand or the potential to win a huge pot. A flop that gives you a set of aces, the nut flush draw and the nut low draw is a big flop and is therefore a through ticket.

Turn - The fourth community card in Omaha and hold 'em.

Up - Used to indicate two pair. A hand consisting of A♥A♦9♣9♠5♠ would be called "aces-up."

Wheel - A 5-high straight. See **Bicycle**.

Wrap - A straight draw that has more than eight outs.

GREAT POKER BOOKS
ADD THESE TO YOUR LIBRARY - ORDER NOW!

TOURNAMENT POKER by Tom McEvoy - Rated by pros as best book on tournaments ever written, and enthusiastically endorsed by more than 5 world champions, this is a must for every player's library. Packed solid with winning strategies for all 11 games in the World Series of Poker, with extensive discussions of 7-card stud, limit hold'em, pot and no-limit hold'em, Omaha high-low, re-buy, half-half tournaments, satellites, strategies for each stage of tournaments. Big player profiles. 344 pages, paperback, $39.95.

OMAHA HI-LO POKER by Shane Smith - Learn essential winning strategies for beating Omaha high-low; the best starting hands, how to play the flop, turn, and river, how to read the board for both high and low, dangerous draws, and how to win low-limit tournaments. Smith shows the differences between Omaha high-low and hold'em strategies. Includes odds charts, glossary, low-limit tips, strategic ideas. 84 pages, 8 x 11, spiral bound, $17.95.

7-CARD STUD (THE COMPLETE COURSE IN WINNING AT MEDIUM & LOWER LIMITS) by Roy West - Learn the latest strategies for winning at $1-$4 spread-limit up to $10-$20 fixed-limit games. Covers starting hands, 3rd-7th street strategy for playing most hands, overcards, selective aggressiveness, reading hands, secrets of the pros, psychology, more - in a 42 "lesson" informal format. Includes bonus chapter on 7-stud tournament strategy by World Champion Tom McEvoy. 160 pages, paperback, $24.95.

POKER TOURNAMENT TIPS FROM THE PROS by Shane Smith - Essential advice from poker theorists, authors, and tournament winners on the best strategies for winning the big prizes at low-limit re-buy tournaments. Learn the best strategies for each of the four stages of play–opening, middle, late and final–how to avoid 26 potential traps, advice on re-buys, aggressive play, clock-watching, inside moves, top 20 tips for winning tournaments, more. Advice from McEvoy, Caro, Malmuth, Ciaffone, others. 102 pages, 8 1/2 x 11, spiral, $19.95.

WINNING LOW LIMIT HOLD'EM by Lee Jones - This essential book on playing 1-4, 3-6, and 1-4-8-8 low limit hold'em is packed with insights on winning: pre-flop positional play; playing the flop in all positions with a pair, two pair, trips, overcards, draws, made and nothing hands; turn and river play; how to read the board; avoiding trash hands; using the check-raise; bluffing, stereotypes, much more. Includes quizzes with answers. Terrific book. 176 pages, 5 1/2 x 8 1/2, paperback, $19.95.

WINNING POKER FOR THE SERIOUS PLAYER by Edwin Silberstang - New edition! More than 100 actual examples provide tons of advice on beating 7 Card Stud, Texas Hold 'Em, Draw Poker, Loball, High-Low and more than 10 other variations. Silberstang analyzes the essentials of being a great player; reading tells, analyzing tables, playing position, mastering the art of deception, creating fear at the table. Also, psychological tactics, when to play aggressive or slow play, or fold, expert plays, more. Colorful glossary included. 288 pages, 6 x 9, perfect bound, $16.95.

WINNER'S GUIDE TO TEXAS HOLD 'EM POKER by Ken Warren - This comprehensive book on beating hold 'em shows serious players how to play every hand from every position with every type of flop. Learn the 14 categories of starting hands, the 10 most common hold 'em tells, how to evaluate a game for profit, and more! Over 50,000 copies in print. 256 pages, 5 1/2 x 8 1/2, paperback, $14.95.

KEN WARREN TEACHES TEXAS HOLD 'EM by Ken Warren - In 33 comprehensive yet easy-to-read chapters, you'll learn absolutely everything about the great game of Texas hold 'em poker. You'll learn to play from every position, at every stage of a hand. You'll master a simple but thorough system for keeping records and understanding odds. And you'll gain expert advice on raising, stealing blinds, avoiding tells, playing for jackpots, bluffing, tournament play, and much more. 416 pages, 6 x 9, $24.95.

Order Toll-Free 1-800-577-WINS or use order form on page 223

THE CHAMPIONSHIP BOOKS
POWERFUL BOOKS YOU MUST HAVE

CHAMPIONSHIP OMAHA (Omaha High-Low, Pot-limit Omaha, Limit High Omaha) by T. J. Cloutier & Tom McEvoy. Clearly-written strategies and powerful advice from Cloutier and McEvoy who have won four World Series of Poker titles in Omaha tournaments. Powerful advice shows you how to win at low-limit and high-stakes games, how to play against loose and tight opponents, and the differing strategies for rebuy and freezeout tournaments. Learn the best starting hands, when slowplaying a big hand is dangerous, what danglers are and why winners don't play them, why pot-limit Omaha is the only poker game where you sometimes fold the nuts on the flop and are correct in doing so and overall, how can you win a lot of money at Omaha! 230 pages, photos, illustrations, $39.95.

CHAMPIONSHIP STUD (Seven-Card Stud, Stud 8/or Better and Razz) by Dr. Max Stern, Linda Johnson, and Tom McEvoy. The authors, who have earned millions of dollars in major tournaments and cash games, eight World Series of Poker bracelets and hundreds of other titles in competition against the best players in the world show you the winning strategies for medium-limit side games as well as poker tournaments and a general tournament strategy that is applicable to any form of poker. Includes give-and-take conversations between the authors to give you more than one point of view on how to play poker. 200 pages, hand pictorials, photos. $29.95.

CHAMPIONSHIP HOLD'EM by T. J. Cloutier & Tom McEvoy. Hard-hitting hold'em the way it's played today in both limit cash games and tournaments. Get killer advice on how to win more money in rammin'-jammin' games, kill-pot, jackpot, shorthanded, and other types of cash games. You'll learn the thinking process before the flop, on the flop, on the turn, and at the river with specific suggestions for what to do when good or bad things happen plus 20 illustrated hands with play-by-play analyses. Specific advice for rocks in tight games, weaklings in loose games, experts in solid games, how hand values change in jackpot games, when you should fold, check, raise, reraise, check-raise, slowplay, bluff, and tournament strategies for small buy-in, big buy-in, rebuy, incremental add-on, satellite and big-field major tournaments. Wow! Easy-to-read and conversational, if you want to become a lifelong winner at limit hold'em, you need this book! 320 Pages, Illustrated, Photos. $39.95

CHAMPIONSHIP NO-LIMIT & POT LIMIT HOLD'EM by T. J. Cloutier & Tom McEvoy The definitive guide to winning at two of the world's most exciting poker games! Written by eight time World Champion players T. J. Cloutier (1998 Player of the Year) and Tom McEvoy (the foremost author on tournament strategy) who have won millions of dollars playing no-limit and pot-limit hold'em in cash games and major tournaments around the world. You'll get all the answers here - no holds barred - to your most important questions: How do you get inside your opponents' heads and learn how to beat them at their own game? How can you tell how much to bet, raise, and reraise in no-limit hold'em? When can you bluff? How do you set up your opponents in pot-limit hold'em so that you can win a monster pot? What are the best strategies for winning no-limit and pot-limit tournaments, satellites, and supersatellites? You get rock-solid and inspired advice from two of the most recognizable figures in poker — advice that you can bank on. If you want to become a winning player, a champion, you must have this book. 209 pages, paperback, illustrations, photos. $39.95

POWERFUL POKER SIMULATIONS
A MUST FOR SERIOUS PLAYERS WITH A COMPUTER!
IBM compatibles CD ROM Windows 3.1, 95, and 98 - Full Color Graphics

Play interactive poker against these **incredible** full color poker simulation programs - they're the absolute **best** method to improve game. Computer players act like real players. All games let you set the limits and rake, have fully programmable players, adjustable lineup, stat tracking, and Hand Analyzer for starting hands. MIke Caro, the world's foremost poker theoretician says, "Amazing...A steal for under $500." Includes free telephone support. **New Feature!** - "Smart advisor" gives expert advice for every play in every game!

1. TURBO TEXAS HOLD'EM FOR WINDOWS - $89.95 - Choose which players, how many, 2-10, you want to play, create loose/tight game, control check-raising, bluffing, position, sensitivity to pot odds, more! Also, instant replay, pop-up odds, Professional Advisor, keeps track of play statistics. Free bonus: Hold'em Hand Analyzer analyzes all 169 pocket hands in detail, their win rates under any conditions you set. Caro says this "hold'em software is the most powerful ever created." Great product!

2. TURBO SEVEN-CARD STUD FOR WINDOWS - $89.95 - Create any conditions of play; choose number of players (2-8), bet amounts, fixed or spread limit, bring-in method, tight/loose conditions, position, reaction to board, number of dead cards, stack deck to create special conditions, instant replay. Terrific stat reporting includes analysis of starting cards, 3-D bar charts, graphs. Play interactively, run high speed simulation to test strategies. Hand Analyzer analyzes starting hands in detail. Wow!

3. TURBO OMAHA HIGH-LOW SPLIT FOR WINDOWS - $89.95 -Specify any playing conditions; betting limits, number of raises, blind structures, button position, aggressiveness/passiveness of opponents, number of players (2-10), types of hands dealt, blinds, position, board reaction, specify flop, turn, river cards! Choose opponents, use provided point count or create your own. Statistical reporting, instant replay, pop-up odds, high speed simulation to test strategies, amazing Hand Analyzer, much more!

4. TURBO OMAHA HIGH FOR WINDOWS - $89.95 - Same features as above, but tailored for the Omaha High-only game. Caro says program is "an electrifying research tool...it can clearly be worth thousands of dollars to any serious player. A must for Omaha High players.

5. TURBO 7 STUD 8 OR BETTER - $89.95 - Brand new with all the features you expect from the Wilson Turbo products: the latest artificial intelligence, instant advice and exact odds, play versus 2-7 opponents, enhanced data charts that can be exported or printed, the ability to fold out of turn and immediately go to the next hand, ability to peek at opponents hand, optional warning mode that warns you if a play disagrees with the advisor, and automatic testing mode that can run up to 50 tests unattended. Challenge tough computer players who vary their styles for a truly great poker game.

---

6. TOURNAMENT TEXAS HOLD'EM - $59.95
Set-up for tournament practice and play, this realistic simulation pits you against celebrity look-alikes. Tons of options let you control tournament size with 10 to 300 entrants, select limits, ante, rake, blind structures, freezeouts, number of rebuys and competition level of opponents - average, tough, or toughest. Pop-up status report shows how you're doing vs. the competition. Save tournaments in progress to play again later. Additional feature allows you to quickly finish a folded hand and go on to the next.

GRI'S PROFESSIONAL VIDEO POKER STRATEGY
Win Money at Video Poker! With the Odds!

At last, for the **first time,** and for **serious players only,** the GRI **Professional Video Poker** strategy is released so you too can play to win! **You read it right** - this strategy gives you the **mathematical advantage** over the casino and what's more, it's **easy to learn!**

PROFESSIONAL STRATEGY SHOWS YOU HOW TO WIN WITH THE ODDS - This **powerhouse strategy,** played for **big profits** by an **exclusive** circle of **professionals,** people who make their living at the machines, is now made available to you! You too can win - with the odds - and this **winning strategy** shows you how!

HOW TO PLAY FOR A PROFIT - You'll learn the **key factors** to play on a **pro level**: which machines will turn you a profit, break-even and win rates, hands per hour and average win per hour charts, time value, team play and more! You'll also learn big play strategy, alternate jackpot play, high and low jackpot play and key strategies to follow.

WINNING STRATEGIES FOR ALL MACHINES - This **comprehensive, advanced pro package** not only shows you how to win money at the 8-5 progressives, but also, the **winning strategies** for 10s or better, deuces wild, joker's wild, flat-top, progressive and special options features.

BE A WINNER IN JUST ONE DAY - In just one day, after learning our strategy, you will have the skills to **consistently win money** at video poker - with the odds. The strategies are easy to use under practical casino conditions.

FREE BONUS - PROFESSIONAL PROFIT EXPECTANCY FORMULA ($15 VALUE) - For serious players, we're including this free bonus essay which explains the professional profit expectancy principles of video poker and how to relate them to real dollars and cents in your game.

To order send just $50 by check or money order to:
Cardoza Publishing, P.O. Box 1500, Cooper Station, New York, NY 10276

GRI'S PROFESSIONAL VIDEO POKER STRATEGY
JUST $50!!! · ORDER NOW!!!

Yes! Please rush me GRI's **Professional Video Poker Strategy** and the **free bonus** ($15 value), **Professional Profit Expectancy Formula.** Enclosed is a check or money order for $50 (plus postage and handling) made out to:
Cardoza Publishing, P.O. Box 1500, Cooper Station, New York, NY 10276

Call Toll-Free in U.S. & Canada, 1-800-577-WINS

Include $5.00 postage/handling for U.S. orders; $10.00 for Canada/Mexico; HI/AK, other countries, $20.00. Outside U.S., money order payable in U.S. dollars on U.S. bank only.

NAME _____

ADDRESS _____

CITY _____ STATE _____ ZIP _____
MC/Visa/Amex Orders By Mail

MC/Visa/Amex# _____ Phone _____

Exp. Date _____ Signature _____
Order Today! 30 Day Money Back Guarantee!   WarrenOmaha

CARDOZA SCHOOL OF BLACKJACK
- Home Instruction Course - $200 OFF! -

At last, after years of secrecy, the **previously unreleased** lesson plans, strategies and playing tactics formerly available only to members of the Cardoza School of Blackjack are now available to the general public - and at substantial savings. **Now**, you can **learn at home,** and at your own convenience. Like the full course given at the school, the home instruction course goes **step-by-ste**p over the winning concepts. We'll take you from layman to **pro.**

MASTER BLACKJACK - Learn what it takes to be a **master player**. Be a **powerhouse**, play with confidence, impunity, and **with the odds** on your side. Learn to be a **big winner** at blackjack.

MAXIMIZE WINNING SESSIONS - You'll **learn how** to take a good winning session and make a **blockbuster** out of it, but just as important, you'll learn to cut your losses. Learn exactly when to end a session. We cover everything from the psychological and emotional aspects of play to altered playing conditions (through the **eye of profitability**) to protection of big wins. The advice here could be worth **hundreds (or thousands) of dollars** in one session alone. Take our guidelines seriously.

ADVANCED STRATEGIES - You'll learn the latest in advanced winning strategies. Learn about the **ten-factor**, the **ace-factor**, the effects of rules variations, how to protect against dealer blackjacks, the winning strategies for single and multiple deck games and how each affects you, the **true count**, the multiple deck true count variations, and much more. And, of course, you'll receive the full Cardoza Base Count Strategy package.

$200 OFF - LIMITED OFFER - The Cardoza School of Blackjack home instruction course, retailed at $295 (or $895 if taken at the school) is available here for just $95.

DOUBLE BONUS! - Rush your order in **now**, for we're also including, **absolutely free**, the 1,000 and 1,500 word essays, "How to Disguise the Fact that You're an Expert", and "How Not to Get Barred". Among other **inside information** contained here, you'll learn about the psychology of the pit bosses, how they spot counters, how to project a losing image, role playing, and other skills to maximize your profit potential.

To order, send $95 (plus postage and handling) by check or money order to:
Cardoza Publishing, P.O. Box 1500, Cooper Station, New York, NY 10276

VIDEOS BY MIKE CARO
THE MAD GENIUS OF POKER

CARO'S PRO POKER TELLS

The long-awaited two-video set is a powerful scientific course on how to use your opponents' gestures, words and body language to read their hands and win all their money. These carefully guarded poker secrets, filmed with 63 poker notables, will revolutionize your game. It reveals when opponents are bluffing, when they aren't, and why. Knowing what your opponent's gestures mean, and protecting them from knowing yours, gives you a huge winning edge. An absolute must buy! $59.95.

CARO'S MAJOR POKER SEMINAR

The legendary "Mad Genius" is at it again, giving poker advice in VHS format. This new tape is based on the inaugural class at Mike Caro University of Poker, Gaming and Life strategy. The material given on this tape is based on many fundamentals introduced in Caro's books, papers, and articles and is prepared in such a way that reinforces concepts old and new. Caro's style is easy-going but intense with key concepts stressed and repeated. This tape will improve your play. 60 Minutes. $24.95.

CARO'S POWER POKER SEMINAR

This powerful video shows you how to win big money using the little-known concepts of world champion players. This advice will be worth thousands of dollars to you every year, even more if you're a big money player! After 15 years of refusing to allow his seminars to be filmed, Caro presents entertaining but serious coverage of his long-guarded secrets. Contains the most profitable poker advice ever put on video. 62 Minutes! $39.95.

Order Toll-Free 1-800-577-WINS or use order form on page 223

CARDOZA PUBLISHING ONLINE

For the latest in poker, gambling, chess, backgammon, and games by the world's top authorities and writers

www.cardozapub.com

To find out about our latest publications and products, to order books and software from third parties, or simply to keep aware of our latest activities in the world or poker, gambling, and other games of chance and skill:

1. Go online: www.cardozapub.com
2. Use E-Mail: cardozapub@aol.com
3. Call toll free: 800-577-WINS (800-577-9467)

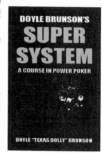